The Unlocking

The Unlocking

God's escape plan for frightened people

Adrian Plass

Published by
The Bible Reading Fellowship
First Floor, Elsfield Hall
15–17 Elsfield Way, Oxford OX2 8FG
ISBN 0 7459 3510 9

First edition 1994
Second edition 1996
10 9 8 7 6 5 4 3 2 1

Acknowledgments
Unless otherwise stated, scripture quotations are taken from the Holy
Bible, New International Version, copyright © 1973, 1978, 1984 by
International Bible Society, are used by permission of Hodder &
Stoughton Limited. All rights reserved. 'NIV' is a registered trademark
of International Bible Society. UK trademark number 1448790.

A catalogue record for this book is available from the British Library

Printed and bound in Great Britain by
Omnia Books Limited, Glasgow

Preface

Writing books is a strange, somewhat neurotic occupation at the best of times—well, it is for me, anyway. I would love to sit serenely in my study, watching the words quietly accumulate in an atmosphere of hushed prayer and deep devotion. I can't. I'm me. I have found the making of many books a tense, grinding, sometimes incredibly exciting business, and I have a feeling it will continue to be like that until the last mouse expires beneath my trembling hand and the final word has been typed.

Worst of all is beginning a book, any book, every book. Seven or eight years ago, Bridget and I took all four of our children to Australia and New Zealand for a four-month speaking tour. The most difficult part of the trip for me was the 500 yards from just outside our house to the top of the road where we had to turn left to set off in the direction of Heathrow Airport. For that short distance I was full of fear. The trip would be a disaster. The children would never recover from missing a term of school. The Australians and New Zealanders would hate everything we said. In fact, it was hardly worth bothering to catch the plane because the whole thing was bound to fail. Five minutes later I was fine, and the reason for my recovery was very simple—we were on our way. It was happening. Starting a book is the same. For a while you know that the stupid, enormous, impossible thing will never get itself written, and then, suddenly, before you know it, you're on your way. It happens.

I mention all these things because the writing of *The Unlocking* was like this, only ten times more so. It was certainly one of the two or three most difficult pieces of work that I have been foolish enough to undertake. It was particularly difficult for two main reasons.

First, I had to write it at speed in the middle of the summer holidays. Crouched over my computer in the corner of a room frequently used by the rest of the family, I was subjected to a constant stream of enquiries as to whether I had finished it yet, and how long it was going to take, and whether there was any point in arranging any family activities for any part of what remained of the holiday, and whether I would come out and play cricket, or golf, or tennis. I had to shut off all receptors to the outside world and get on with it.

The second problem was that I had committed myself to being as grittily truthful as possible about the many fears that I experience, in order that readers might be able to identify readily with aspects of my vulnerability. I groaned and procrastinated and fiddled and messed about, trying to find some way to escape the consequences of this personal commitment, but it was not to be escaped. Writing that book was like tearing some inner lining out of myself and sticking it down on paper. What a disgusting image, and what a very accurate one.

Was it worth it? Well, that was why I wanted to write a preface to this revised edition of *The Unlocking*. I don't think any other book that I have written has produced such a positive response. By that I mean that many, many people have been kind enough to let me know, by various means, just how closely they have identified with the parts of my troubled nature explored in the book, and how comforted they have felt by the realization that they are *not alone*. What more could a writer ask for?

We who follow Jesus are all on the same journey. That is what this book is about. We fall and we stand and we walk and we fall again and we lean on the arm of another, and they in their turn lean on us, and eventually we shall all arrive together at the Holy City where there will be no more fears and no more falling. We shall hug Jesus and he will hug us and we shall all hug each other and almost instantaneously we shall be free, and we shall forget what locks were for.

Adrian Plass

Contents

This book is dedicated with much love to my friend,
Daidie Wincott, who has known a lot of fear, and
shown a lot of courage.

Introduction

I am a frightened person. God began the unlocking process in me a long time ago, and it's still going on today. I'm sure that God *wants* to tackle the fears that cripple us. The resurrection of Jesus made all things possible and the Holy Spirit moves in our lives with all the ingenuity of the Creator God. That doesn't actually make it any easier to identify methods or techniques. God has as many solutions as there are people with fears, and they're all going to be different.

So what can we do? What will different solutions have in common? What is God's plan for frightened people?

I think the first part of the answer is that members of the body of Christ need to learn to depend on each other much more than has been the case in the recent years of feverishly pursued individual spiritual achievement. You'll read a lot about that in this book.

Secondly, in every case I know of where fear has been overcome, an essential truth has become stronger than that fear. Jesus summed it up: 'Then you will know the truth, and the truth will set you free.'

That's it in a nutshell, but, as you know, some nutshells are very hard to crack. Let's have a go, though.

Each of the pieces you're about to read begins with a look at the truth as it's given to us by God in the Bible. I'll then respond to the passage as honestly as I can, hoping that as many readers as possible will identify with my ravings! (Do feel free to laugh *or* cry.) Then I'll invite you to join me in praying from the heart about the issues that have arisen. The book was originally written for Lent studies, and is arranged in sections, but please don't fall into the trap of thinking that you've got to stick to a particular one, or that you'll lose your salvation if you skip one of the pieces. Use the book in any way you want. My dearest wish is that, as you read, you'll forget about me, and just be close to this wonderful God of ours.

By the way, the other essential ingredient is obedience. If, after talking to him, he tells you to do something, for goodness' sake do it! Don't worry if it seems strange or 'not quite your style'—just do it!

God bless you as you join me now, and I pray from the bottom of my heart that something in this book will begin the process of releasing you from your fear. Let the unlocking begin.

Where we begin

The desert and the devil

Then Jesus was led by the Spirit into the desert to be tempted by the devil. After fasting for forty days and forty nights, he was hungry. The tempter came to him and said, 'If you are the Son of God, tell these stones to become bread.' Jesus answered, 'It is written: "Man does not live on bread alone, but on every word that comes from the mouth of God."' Then the devil took him to the holy city and had him stand on the highest point of the temple. 'If you are the Son of God,' he said, 'throw yourself down. For it is written: "He will command his angels concerning you, and they will lift you up in their hands, so that you will not strike your foot against a stone."' Jesus answered him, 'It is also written: "Do not put the Lord your God to the test."' Again, the devil took him to a very high mountain and showed him all the kingdoms of the world and their splendour. 'All this I will give you,' he said, 'if you will bow down and worship me.' Jesus said to him, 'Away from me, Satan! For it is written: "Worship the Lord your God, and serve him only."' Then the devil left him, and angels came and attended him.

MATTHEW 4:1–11

For those of us who value our salvation (and there are a few of us still roaming the Jurassic Park of Christendom) it is worth reflecting that during this period of forty days the whole salvation plan could have failed completely. Jesus was truly man, and therefore must have been capable of giving in to temptation. If this was not so, his ministry in general, and these forty days in particular, become a nonsense.

The Gospel accounts of this crucial event are fairly brief, and can't even begin to convey the agony of mind, body and spirit that Jesus must have endured as he wrestled with temptations to use selfishly the incredible power that now flooded through him. We can discard the mental picture of a tall, noble, clear-eyed, blond hero with a tame cherubim perched on his shoulder like a chubby parrot, dismissing Satan with an airy wave of the hand. After almost six weeks of fasting in the heat of the desert, reviewing again and again the fatal implications of total commitment to his Father, Jesus, thin and weary, must have come seriously close to adopting the way of the world and the devil. Material possessions, personal safety and ultimate power were set before him like a three-runged ladder to earthly contentment. In his weakened state it must have seemed a very attractive option compared to three years of celibacy, conflict and rejection, followed by one of the most painful forms of execution ever devised by man. Jesus didn't give in to temptation. He flung scriptural truths at the devil, rather as David flung stones at Goliath. And the comparison is a fair one. Jesus had to win this battle as a real man supported by God, even though he was also God, so that it could be possible for him to say to ordinary men and women, 'Be perfect, even as I am perfect.' It is a mystery beyond mysteries, but, like many mysteries, it quite easily finds a home in the secret heart of our understanding.

There is a profound fear in many Christians that they will fail in their own wilderness experience. At one time or another each of us is asked to walk into the desert and face the question about where our final commitment lies. It feels awfully dark to give away the world and all that it might offer, but it is the beginning of ministry. Jesus was armed with knowledge of the Scriptures, and (as long as we don't get silly about it) so should we be. He also walked *voluntarily* into that desert. God doesn't push people into the wilderness, but if we find ourselves there he might well suggest that the time has come to make the most basic choice of all.

Have I made that choice? Well, I've certainly been in a desert or two, and I've seen the options lined up before me quite clearly. I've tried to dismiss the devil, with only partial success, but opportunities are still graciously offered to me by God, and Jesus died to bridge the gap between what I am and what I should be, so I remain optimistic.

The thing I'm really looking forward to, if I ever do finally resist Satan, is the bit where the angels appear with a bottle of lemonade and a packet of sandwiches.

The way we were

'I tell you, whoever acknowledges me before men, the Son of Man will also acknowledge him before the angels of God. But he who disowns me before men will be disowned before the angels of God.'
LUKE 12:8–9

When I first became a Christian at the age of sixteen I did some ridiculous things. Once, at a Christian youth club a few miles from my home, I literally bullied some poor, mild non-Christian into a back room and on to his knees, so that he could make a commitment using a prayer dictated by my good self. I can still see his wild, staring eyes as he was pitchforked into the Kingdom by a tall, skinny (yes, I said skinny) fanatic who wasn't going to take 'No' for an answer. If, by some miracle of God's grace, that fellow is a Christian today, and he's reading this—I do apologize. I wouldn't do that today.

Customers in the coffee-drinking dens of Tunbridge Wells must have got pretty fed up with me too. Armed with my regulation-issue Bible and burning enthusiasm, I would harangue anyone and everyone about the need to 'get right with God'. Sensitivity didn't come into it. I told them about Jesus whether they wanted to hear or not. Of course, I wouldn't do it like that now.

Later, when I was eighteen or nineteen, I went off to theatre school in Bristol, accompanied by the same Bible and the same attitude. I clutched that Bible to me like Linus clutches his blanket. Poor old Bristolians. The scruffy evangelist was among them, still cornering people in bars and cafés and on public transport, and enquiring about the state of their souls. Naturally, I would approach it all very differently today.

Later still, I found myself working with children who had educational problems, at a boarding school in Gloucestershire. My zeal had abated a little, but I almost didn't get the job because I said I was a 'born-again Christian' on the application form.

One day, I was playing cricket with one of the boys in a practice net at the edge of the field. He hit the ball out of the net and into some bushes. We looked for ages, but with no luck. Finally, I said to him, 'We'll pray about it, shall we?'

'Eh?' said the boy.

'I'll ask God to find the ball for us.'

'Eh?'

'Father, we know you're interested in little things, so will you please help us to find our ball?'

When I opened my eyes I looked down and saw that the ball was lying on the ground between the boy's feet. His eyes nearly fell out of his head. I was really pleased to see the ball, but, of course, I wouldn't approach a similar situation in that naïve way nowadays.

Last week, I was trying to get a car boot open for a friend. We tugged and fiddled and prised and pulled and pushed, but nothing made any difference. As I knelt at the back of the car, clean out of options, it occurred to me that I could ask God to help us. I did ask him silently, but something told me that only an 'out-loud' prayer was going to be any use here. I chickened out. I publicly acknowledge Jesus all the time, but I'm a bit out of practice when it comes to the private sector.

I did do a lot of very silly things when I was a young Christian, and I'm sure a lot of people found me a real pain in the neck, but I feel sad when I compare my readiness to tell everybody that my life belonged to Jesus, and that theirs ought to as well, with the way I speak to people now. I think I've got a bit frightened of being simple about my faith in ordinary situations, and, now that I've read this passage again, I think I ought to do something about it.

Pray with me

Father, I feel a bit of a fool when I look back at those early years, but there was a sort of childlike passion in me then that just overflowed all the time. I certainly don't want to be that particular kind of idiot again, but I wouldn't mind being a different kind of idiot now. I want to be ready to acknowledge you openly and enthusiastically at the right time, and to be sensitive enough to know when it's the wrong time. It's ridiculous that I should be frightened of using your Son's name after all these years. Perhaps I need to fall in love with him all over again. Grant me a fresh vision of your love, Lord, a new excitement that can't help communicating itself to others. Thank you. Amen.

Power steering

But whatever was to my profit I now consider loss for the sake of Christ. What is more, I consider everything a loss compared to the surpassing greatness of knowing Christ Jesus my Lord, for whose sake I have lost all things. I consider them rubbish, that I may gain Christ and be found in him, not having a righteousness of my own that comes from the law, but that which is through faith in Christ—the righteousness that comes from God and is by faith. I want to know Christ and the power of his resurrection and the fellowship of sharing in his sufferings, becoming like him in his death, and so, somehow, to attain to the resurrection from the dead.

PHILIPPIANS 3:7–11

I do envy Paul the boldness and enthusiasm of his statements about Jesus. He really is sold out, isn't he? Nothing is worth hanging on to if it isn't Christ; everything is rubbish compared to knowing him; and if suffering is part of the package, he welcomes it because he wants to share his Master's suffering. His life's work consists of up-front, full-blooded, evangelistic reaching out to anyone who will listen to the good news of salvation. I wish I was like him, but I'm not.

It's not just that I don't have the same kind of confidence in God, although that certainly is a major difference between Paul and myself (every now and then I have hot flushes of total doubt). It's also that I get very worried about someone as spiritually and morally fragile as I am trying to tell other people what they should think or feel about Jesus. In between the aforementioned hot flushes, I do have a real passion for God and, like a mini-Jeremiah, I would seriously singe my bones if I didn't let it out, but I fear my own presumption in doing so. Many of my fellow purveyors of spiritual 'stuff' will know exactly what I mean. Fortunately, the Holy Spirit has very recently suggested a metaphor, unavailable to Paul, that I've found very helpful. (I was about to press the delete button on 'Holy Spirit' and replace it with 'a great deal of thought'. I repented and left it as it was.) So here, for all those who fear that proselytizing looks like pride, is a suggestion that we are nothing but 'chauffeurs':

Yeah, took this job on eight years ago—read about it somewhere. Didn't think I'd get it, but I did. Training on the job—all equipment provided. Long hours, but a day off a week. He insisted on that. Weekday usually—haven't had a Sunday off in years. Wages? Well, a bit odd really. All expenses paid, but the rest comes in a lump sum at the end. I trust him. He'll pay up.

Duties? Well, basically driving the boss anywhere and everywhere he wants to go. Little meetings, big meetings, people in houses, people in the street, he says where and I just take him. Good man, the boss. More like family now. Been very good to me, one way and another. Likes a joke and a laugh, but I tell you what—you wouldn't want to cross him. Uniform's got to be just so, car's got to be clean, reliable, and always topped up ready to go. I mustn't drive too slow, mustn't go over the speed limit, but *must* get him there on time. And another thing, *he* decides on the route and the destination, and that's that. Took him what I thought was a better way once and when we got there I turned round and he'd got out! Don't know when or where, but he'd just gone. Embarrassed? Not half! They were all waiting for him to talk in this hall so I had to pretend to be him. Not very impressed, they weren't. Never tried it on again.

Dangerous? Yeah, sometimes we've been into very nasty areas indeed—only when he says, mind, but it has got quite scary at times. Glad I'm only the chauffeur in some of them places. You feel sort of safe with the boss there, though—difficult to imagine anything he couldn't handle. He's got that certain something about him. Good with people.

Proud of my job? Yeah, I suppose I am really—well, proud of being involved in what he does, even if I only drive him. Tell you what, it gives me a good feeling opening the door when we get somewhere and seeing all the people get excited when he steps out. Sort of reflected glory, if you know what I mean. I always stand well back so everyone can get a good first look at him. Feel proud then. Proud of him, I mean. Yeah, *very* proud of him.

Pray with me

Lord Jesus, you have an enormous number of people like us working for you and with you. We do different jobs and we have different problems and responsibilities but, in the end, we all answer to you. Whatever the individual task is, help us to see that we are jointly involved in the urgent business of offering you, and the salvation you bought for us, to a lost world. We don't want to get in the way, but we don't want to get so far out of the way that we aren't doing anything at all. We are fearful people and we tend to focus on our inadequacy and unworthiness. Let us see and understand the nature of the contribution that you want us to make, however humble that is, and, like your servant, Paul, feel a proper pride in being associated with you—the boss. Amen.

Death, thou shalt die

Jesus said to her, 'I am the resurrection and the life. He who believes in me will live, even though he dies; and whoever lives and believes in me will never die. Do you believe this?' 'Yes, Lord,' she told him, 'I believe that you are the Christ, the Son of God, who was to come into the world.'
JOHN 11:25–27

When they heard this, they were furious and gnashed their teeth at him. But Stephen, full of the Holy Spirit, looked up to heaven and saw the glory of God, and Jesus standing at the right hand of God. 'Look,' he said, 'I see heaven open and the Son of Man standing at the right hand of God.' At this they covered their ears and, yelling at the top of their voices, they all rushed at him, dragged him out of the city and began to stone him. Meanwhile, the witnesses laid their clothes at the feet of a young man named Saul. While they were stoning him, Stephen prayed, 'Lord Jesus, receive my spirit.' Then he fell on his knees and cried out, 'Lord, do not hold this sin against them.' When he had said this, he fell asleep.
ACTS 7:54–60

On the first day of the week we came together to break bread. Paul spoke to the people and, because he intended to leave the next day, kept on talking until midnight. There were many lamps in the upstairs room where we were meeting. Seated in a window was a young man named Eutychus, who was sinking into a deep sleep as Paul talked on and on. When he was sound asleep, he fell to the ground from the third storey and was picked up dead. Paul went down, threw himself on the young man and put his arms around him. 'Don't be alarmed,' he said. 'He's alive!' Then he went upstairs again and broke bread and ate. After talking until daylight, he left. The people took the young man home alive and were greatly comforted.
ACTS 20:7–12

I have always been frightened of death. As a small child of seven or so, I lay in my bed at night wondering how I would ever manage if my parents died. I knew that people did die, because my beloved grandmother had done it when I was six, and I could still feel the cold, heavy weight of grief in my stomach every time I thought about her. My mother said she was in heaven and I would see her again one day, so that was good, but I couldn't bear the thought of anyone else going on ahead without me. Sometimes I couldn't sleep for worrying about it, and I would call my mother through to sit on the end of my bed and tell me that everything was all right. In the morning it always *was* all right—mornings and death just didn't go together—but by the time night came again the worry was back, filling my mind with a deeper darkness even than the darkness of my room. I *hated* death. What was the point of living if we were all going to die? My small soul *raged* against death. A proper little Dylan Thomas, I was.

That fear never left me as I grew older. Indeed, it grew worse, because the stuff about heaven was no longer very convincing. The inevitable fact of death was a heavy blanket smothering any chance of a final surrender to joy. Know the feeling?

The message of these words of Jesus, recorded in the eleventh chapter of John's Gospel, was the ray of hope that first lightened the gloom in my soul. The voice that spoke them was filled with natural authority, despite the fact that it was speaking through the printed page. With the coming of Jesus, I discovered, death had been taken by the scruff of the neck, shaken like a rat, and, through Jesus' crucifixion and resurrection, completely defeated. Now, as the second and third passages above show (I could have selected many examples), the movement between living and dying had become fluid, reversible, and, in the eternal sense, irrelevant. The book of Acts is full of an immense excitement among those early followers of Christ, as they tested and witnessed the power of this new principle in their own lives. Do read Acts like a novel—it's wonderful!

I still hate and rage against death. I hate it because it causes such devastating grief, and leaves such loneliness, and hurts people physically so much sometimes. I cannot sing choruses at the graveside, and

I don't think Jesus could have done either. He was too sane. But I do know in my heart of hearts that, on the most important level, there is no need to fear now. The man who died for my sins has overcome death, and God is in control.

What would I say if something dreadful happened to one of my children? The answer is that I don't know. I don't *know* why he allows such awful things to happen sometimes, but I do know that the pain we feel is felt by him as well, and I'm not going to wrap up such issues in pretty platitudes. Jesus never did. He is in it with us.

Pray with me

Jesus, many of us have known such pain through the death of people we love.

Some of us are resentful. We don't want to be, but we are. We want to know why you didn't do anything about it when we prayed so hard for so long. What was the point, Lord? What was the point? You say you love us, and then you break our hearts by taking away someone who meant everything to us. What was the point of it?

Some of us are still very unsure about heaven and salvation and all that. Is it absolutely definite that it's going to be all right? Is everything in the Bible true? Will you be waiting for us when we get there? Will you, Lord?

Some of us are very scared of the pain of dying, Jesus. We wake up in a cold sweat sometimes, filled with the dread of a long, pain-filled illness. Will you be with us if that happens, Lord? We will listen to your calm, strong voice again, Lord, and take heart: 'I am the resurrection and the life. He who believes in me will live, even though he dies; and whoever lives and believes in me will never die. Do you believe this?'

Lord Jesus, thank you for dying on our behalf. Receive and forgive our shouts of anger, pain, confusion and fear. We do believe—help our unbelief. Amen.

Friends

But Ruth replied, 'Don't urge me to leave you or to turn back from you. Where you go I will go, and where you stay I will stay. Your people will be my people and your God my God. Where you die I will die, and there I will be buried. May the Lord deal with me, be it ever so severely, if anything but death separates you and me.' When Naomi realized that Ruth was determined to go with her, she stopped urging her. So the two women went on until they came to Bethlehem. When they arrived in Bethlehem, the whole town was stirred because of them, and the women exclaimed, 'Can this be Naomi?' 'Don't call me Naomi,' she told them. 'Call me Mara, because the Almighty has made my life very bitter.'
RUTH 1:16–20

The book of Ruth is a fresh, invigorating breeze amid the dramatic, turbulent storms of the Old Testament. The characters in it are such *nice* people. I would love to have known Ruth and Naomi and Boaz. But they are also very ordinary, human people, and in this passage we find Naomi almost giving in to a quite illusory fear that God has left her with nothing in this world.

She had lost an awful lot, of course. The death of a husband and two sons would be a tragedy in any age, but in that country at that time it was utter disaster. Nevertheless, the fact was that the Lord had not brought Naomi back 'empty' to her home town of Bethlehem. Standing beside her, even as she said those words, was a daughter-in-law who simply could not have been more devoted and loving. Ruth could have gone back to Moab and the safety of her relatives, but instead she stayed with her mother-in-law. I wonder if the young widow was a little hurt by Naomi's total despair.

Some months ago, my wife had a phone call from a very old friend of ours who lives in Scotland with his wife and two children. They're a lovely family. Both Ted and Sally have been in full-time youth work for years and are highly skilled in that area. Every now and then, though, crises accumulate in their lives like poison under the skin, and when the 'burst' comes they usually travel down to visit us. We've 'used' them in the same way sometimes. This time they really had reached a point of despair, and as we sat around the kitchen table watching the children play in the yard outside, Ted was in a dark mood.

'We feel as a family that God has deserted us,' he said gloomily. 'We've been left alone and helpless.'

I was well into my nodding-sympathetically-and-saying-I-know-what-you-mean routine when it suddenly occurred to me that Ted was talking utter garbage. Here we all were, Ted and Sally and Bridget and I, a little unit of the body of Christ, supporting each other as we had done for years, and it was possible because God had given us to each other for this very purpose a long time ago. It took poor old Ted a little while to appreciate this point, of course. It's always a bit annoying to be told that your misery doesn't need to be quite as profound as you had thought it did!

When we do reach these rock-bottom times in our lives, it's well worth sparing a moment to recognize how much God has given us in terms of close, supportive friends or family. Sometimes the very person to whom we express our desolation is the greatest gift we have ever received. It is an awe-inspiring thought that when we touch the hand of a fellow Christian we are touching the body of Jesus on earth.

As for Naomi—well, it was through Ruth that she found a new family, new hope, and a little child called Obed to love and look after. Later, that child was to be the grandfather of David, king of Israel and a man after God's own heart. God did not bring her back empty, did he?

Pray with me

Father, I'm going to take a few minutes to think through the names of people who have been close to me over the years. I know I take some of them for granted, and don't even connect them with you. Thank you so much for their love, and your kindness in giving them to me. Forgive me for accusing you of deserting me when you have always been present in them. It must hurt you very much.

I know, Father, that some people really do have no one special in their lives. They fear that you don't care. I want to assure you that I will try to be sensitive to the voice of the Spirit when he speaks to me about another part of the Body that needs your presence through mine. Amen.

Fear of failure

Opening up

This is the message we have heard from him and declare to you: God is light; in him there is no darkness at all. If we claim to have fellowship with him yet walk in the darkness, we lie and do not live by the truth. But if we walk in the light, as he is in the light, we have fellowship with one another, and the blood of Jesus, his Son, purifies us from every sin. 1 JOHN 1:5–7

Quite often, when I'm speaking to a group of people, I begin with a few comments about myself.

'First of all,' I might announce, 'I'm a failed Christian. Any other failed Christians here?'

In the churches where we are supposed to be a triumphant army marching to victory, a slight hiatus occurs at this point, but it only needs a couple of brave and honest hands to be raised for everyone else to realize that vulnerability can't kill you.

'Let's face it,' I usually add, 'we're all a load of ratbags when it comes down to it, aren't we?'

Very occasionally some highly respectable churchgoer will flush and bristle at the indignity of being described in this manner, but, generally speaking, a gentle wave of relaxation and relief ripples through the gathering of saints. It's not going to be one of *those* evenings.

Mind you, bringing our weaknesses into the light can be a terribly painful experience. I remember, all too vividly, an evening which occurred some years ago, not long after I had taken on a new job working with children in the care of the local authority. It had become abundantly clear that most of the members of the staff group I was supposed to be leading were not at all happy with the way I was doing my job. Their unhappiness was probably justified in many ways, but that wasn't really the point. The point was that the criticism was unspoken (as far as I was concerned), and that it was beginning to poison the atmosphere of the unit in which we all worked.

It felt essential to create an opportunity for the unspoken to be spoken. I invited the entire staff group to my house one evening, gave each of them a drink, and suggested that they should tell me exactly where they believed I was going wrong. This they proceeded to do— most of them—in some detail and at some length. Afterwards, when everyone had gone, I cried. It was probably most unwise voluntarily to provoke such a barrage of personal complaint, but I do know that things began to improve from that day onwards. There is something about voicing criticism openly that forces critics to look more closely at their own weaknesses.

We are all ratbags, and that's what this passage is about. Of course, habitual and intentional evil is a component of walking in darkness, but, for most of us, problems occur when we won't allow the light to shine on quite ordinary problems, sins and deficiencies. When we, as members of the Body of Christ, are ruefully, humorously, sometimes tearfully honest with each other, there is forgiveness in the very air that we breathe.

When I was abroad some years ago I met a Christian who had wrestled all his life with the most perverse of sexual temptations. I was the first person, other than close family and counsellors, to whom he had revealed his problem. I have never before seen such an amalgam of mental, spiritual and physical pain as that man suffered in this act of self-revelation. It hurt him and it challenged me, but in that moment of confession the light burst through, and we were in true fellowship.

Pray with me

Lord, I would like to be more vulnerable, but I'll tell you what really troubles me. If I open up and talk about myself, will other people do the

Born guilty

If we claim to be without sin, we deceive ourselves and the truth is not in us. If we confess our sins, he is faithful and just and will forgive us our sins and purify us from all unrighteousness. If we claim we have not sinned, we make him out to be a liar and his word has no place in our lives.

1 JOHN 1:8–10

I once knew a man who, for a time, espoused the 'health, wealth and sinlessness' movement. When his eyesight began to fail he refused to wear glasses, because to do so would reveal lack of faith in God's healing promise. Unfortunately he continued to drive a car while he was waiting for this miracle, and a number of local citizens were drawn into sins of cursing and ill temper by the near-collisions that resulted. The wealth side of things didn't go too well either, I seem to recall, and if he stayed sinless in the face of all that, he doesn't belong in this world.

That man apart, I don't think I've ever met anyone who seriously claimed to be without sin. I have, however, met two other kinds of people.

First, there are those who'll freely admit to being guilty of faults and vices, but see no connection between human shortcomings and a God they probably don't believe in anyway. Their sins, they would say, are not much different from anyone else's, and, of course, they're right. What they don't see is the potentially disastrous gap between themselves and God, caused by the sin of humankind, as opposed to that of any individual. God help us to find more effective ways to communicate this urgent truth than some of the expensively ineffective ones we've used in the past.

The other kind of people are those who put on a sort of guilt suit every morning. This is nothing to do with conviction of sin and repentance. It is to do with being so obsessed by the probability of failure that we lose sight of the fact that Jesus died precisely so that we could find peace. I'm afraid church groups can be less than helpful in this area. Here is a *slightly* exaggerated version of what happens:

Leader: *(With soupy-eyed gloom)* I thought we might pass this evening, if we are spared until ten o'clock, by reminding each other of our miserable sinful state. Let us commence by sharing any insights into our verminous natures that have been vouchsafed to us in the week that has passed. Mona, perhaps you would begin?

Mona: No, I am not worthy.

Leader: Henry, might you…?

Henry: I am even less worthy.

Leader: Elspeth?

Elspeth: I am an abomination.

Leader: Jerome?

Jerome: I should be spread upon a pond.
(Pause)

Leader: Perhaps the least worthy…?
(Chorus of 'Me! Me! I should start! Let me be the one!' etc)

Jerome: I am in possession of a small, self-denigrating anecdote.

Leader: Proceed.

Jerome: On Monday I perceived a humble slug crushed by some unheeding boot upon the pathway, and I reflected on the fact that this demised creature was a much greater contributor to the work of the kingdom than a wretch such as I shall ever be.

Leader: Did you repent of your self-absorption?

Jerome: Indeed, with avidity.

Mona: How do those cope who know not such joy as ours?

Henry: With ease compared to our poor efforts if we were in like state, I would submit…

What nonsense, but wherever the sheer *niceness* of God is unacknowledged, you will find folk who really are crippled by guilt. To those people, I believe God gently says, 'I understand how you feel, but I'm more concerned with your refusal to accept my gift to you than I ever was with those things you gloom over every day. Read about the prodigal son, children—and lighten up.'

Pray with me

I've read the story of the prodigal son, Father, and I realize that, as far as you're concerned, repentance is a joyful thing. We confess our sins and you throw your arms round us. Big party—great stuff! But, Lord, some of us are diseased with this guilt thing. We've grown up with it, we're weighed down with it, we can't get rid of it. Far from saying we have no sin, we don't accept forgiveness when it's offered to us. We need to come within the orbit of your fondness, Father—to know that the wanting of us is really real. We need to feel clean as well as being clean. Thank you for being so nice. Work a little miracle so we can believe that, as well as saying it. Then we shall have something to say to the ones who don't connect their sin with you at all. Amen.

Cry from the heart

O Lord, the God who saves me, day and night I cry out before you. May my prayer come before you; turn your ear to my cry. For my soul is full of trouble and my life draws near the grave. I am counted among those who go down to the pit; I am like a man without strength. I am set apart with the dead, like the slain who lie in the grave, whom you remember no more, who are cut off from your care. You have put me in the lowest pit, in the darkest depths. Your wrath lies heavily upon me; you have overwhelmed me with all your waves.

PSALM 88:1–7

Unlike most of the Psalms, this shout of pain begins and ends with darkness. The only hint of optimism lies in the writer's obvious belief that there is some point in addressing all these desperate sentiments to a God who is in control of his salvation, and might listen—or even *do* something if he feels so inclined.

We seem, in this age, to have forgotten what it means to batter on the doors of heaven. Depression, bad health and continuous ill-fortune have the effect of drying up communication with God, perhaps because there is a feeling nowadays that polite enthusiasm and trampolining exhortation are the only legitimate modes of prayer.

The person who wrote this psalm was reaching towards heaven from his sickbed or his circumstances, to grasp the attention of God (whom he respected in the most practical sense) with an outpouring of anguish that is undiluted by watery religion. There really is nothing wrong with telling God exactly how we feel.

Once, in the middle of a meeting, I felt that it would be useful for some people to spend a few minutes 'forgiving God' for what he had done or failed to do in their lives. Of course, I added, he hasn't actually done anything wrong, but that's the problem. Resentment

34

and disappointment fester when they're allowed no expression, and the God I know is quite able to handle the hurt that we feel, especially if it's directed safely towards him. A year later I met a lady who described how that few minutes of straightness with God had revolutionized her relationship with him.

There's only one rule about addressing God, especially when our lives seem to be failing completely. Speak from the heart—like a child...

I am less than one year old.

Just now when I was feeling really bad some people came to my house and carried me outside to a white lorry. My daddy *gave* me to them even though I felt really, really poorly. He helped them put me in the lorry and then he got in as well. After a lot of bumping we have come to a very big house full of people in white clothes. Daddy left me with a lady who I don't know and she did things to me that I didn't like. Daddy *let* her! Then Daddy came back, but only for a very little while, and he didn't even hold me or look at me because his hands were over his face. Different people keep coming in and staring at me. I am very hungry but Daddy hasn't brought me any dinner. I feel even more poorly than I did when Daddy gave me to those men. *Why* did he do that? I don't know what will happen next. I don't like it here and my head feels funny and I don't understand why Daddy doesn't take me home and stop the hurting. Why doesn't he care about me any more? When he comes back in I'm going to cry and cry and cry and cry...

Pray with me

Father, a lot of us have been holding in some very strong feelings for a long time. We haven't been sure how you would react to hearing what we'd say if we ever let it all out. If it's really true that you don't mind us being absolutely open with you, then help us to open our mouths and release the anger or unhappiness or resentment or whatever it is in your direction. Some of us want to climb up on your knee and batter your chest like little children, and maybe even say, 'I hate you! I hate you! I hate you!' Small children usually cry when they've done that, and then they fall asleep cuddled up on the lap of the person they've been shouting at. Oh, Father! Some of us need to do that so badly. Will you help us now, please? Amen.

Helping the helpless

But I cry to you for help, O Lord; in the morning my prayer comes before you. Why, O Lord, do you reject me and hide your face from me? From my youth I have been afflicted and close to death; I have suffered your terrors and am in despair. Your wrath has swept over me; your terrors have destroyed me. All day long they surround me like a flood; they have completely engulfed me. You have taken my companions and loved ones from me; the darkness is my closest friend.

PSALM 88:13–18

How do you cope with someone who is in such darkness? I don't think this chap's problem is going to be solved by a tract, or a relevant verse, or even a Christian paperback, do you?

I am not a stranger to the kind of flooding despair that this writer is talking about, and I am not at all surprised that his friends and neighbours are shunning him. I can tell you from personal experience that what counts is not what people say, nor what they give you materially, nor even what they do exactly, but what they *are*. You very soon find out what an individual's faith means when he or she is faced with someone else's dissolution.

Some people panic. They want the problem solved, cleared up, got rid of as soon as possible because raggedness threatens the artificially tidy, religious construct that helps them to feel secure. Putting plasters on badly wounded people to make yourself feel better is not very helpful.

Others are determined to search out the underlying cause of the problem, convinced that if they could just work out exactly what to lay hands on, or cast out, or pray through to victory for, then all would be well. There's nothing wrong with searching, of course, but what if you find nothing?

The friends who were most helpful to me were those who didn't need to have all the ends tied up, the ones who were content with a mystery, the ones who weren't seeking to solve some problem of their own through my recovery, the ones who were happy to be the hands of God without insisting on active involvement with the brain, the ones who were simply *there* beside me when I needed them.

Thank God for the willing foot-soldiers.

Pray with me

Lord, help us to bring the same disinterested, non-judgmental compassion to our failing, falling friends as Mother Teresa's 'sisters' bring to those starving beggars in whom they see Jesus.

We must learn to control the panic that rises in us when we are confronted by pain and insecurity in others. We know they need love rather than religion, but sometimes their darkness infects the light in us and we want to shut the door on them after chucking a verse or an admonition or a warning or a 'God bless you' in their general direction. Father, we want to be more like Jesus, whose love was always tailored to individual needs. The cost will be high. We know that. Help us not to be mean and cowardly. Amen.

Towards more beautiful music

We who are strong ought to bear with the failings of the weak and not to please ourselves. Each of us should please his neighbour for his good, to build him up. For even Christ did not please himself but, as it is written, 'The insults of those who insult you have fallen on me.' For everything that was written in the past was written to teach us, so that through endurance and the encouragement of the Scriptures we might have hope. May the God who gives endurance and encouragement give you a spirit of unity among yourselves as you follow Christ Jesus, so that with one heart and mouth you may glorify the God and Father of our Lord Jesus Christ.

ROMANS 15:1–6

As I read this passage I scratched my head and asked the following question. Am I one of the weak, whose failings ought to be put up with, or am I one of the strong, who ought to put up with the failings of the weak? Doesn't scripture indicate that if I think I'm strong, I'm almost certainly weak, and that if I believe I'm weak, then I'm probably strong? And if I think I'm strong, shouldn't people put up with my failings, because I'm actually weak? And shouldn't I put my head in a concrete bucket and sing nursery rhymes to the moon?

Do you get into spiritual knots like this? I have a particular talent for it. In fact, like so many of these apparent tangles, it straightens out as soon as we introduce the neglected concept of 'kindness'. I am both weak and strong (like most of us), and I need the kind forbearance of my brothers and sisters as I broadcast my conviction that only people in vine costumes will be allowed to enter heaven, or whatever the current obsession happens to be. I hope friends will gently talk me out of the loonier ideas, but each phase can feel terribly important at the time.

Conversely I, in particular, need to learn respect for the tenderness of other people's principles and abstinences, especially when they appear to have more of an imprisoning effect than a freeing one. You can't bully folk out of being what they are (although you might laugh them into a slightly different shape sometimes).

Pray with me

This is a hard lesson, Lord. What you seem to be saying is that anything I do, no matter how splendid or significant I, or anyone else, might think it, is useless if it fails to contribute to the harmony that should exist between members of the Body of Christ. I don't mind admitting in theory that I'm weak, but I have to confess a real fear of appearing weak in certain situations. I also have to admit that I've quite often found myself talking disparagingly about fellow Christians because the things they're doing or saying seem weak and foolish, and don't fit in with my idea of how the Church should be. Forgive us for the times when we make these comments that are almost invariably unconstructive, and hurtful to the Holy Spirit. Forgive our arrogance towards people whom you love. We do want the one voice of the Church to be a happy and harmonious one. Amen.

Pushing the limits

Now the body is not made up of one part but of many. If the foot should say, 'Because I am not a hand, I do not belong to the body,' it would not for that reason cease to be part of the body. And if the ear should say, 'Because I am not an eye, I do not belong to the body,' it would not for that reason cease to be part of the body. If the whole body were an eye, where would the sense of hearing be? If the whole body were an ear, where would the sense of smell be? But in fact God has arranged the parts in the body, every one of them, just as he wanted them to be. If they were all one part, where would the body be? As it is, there are many parts, but one body.

1 CORINTHIANS 12:14–20

There is a freedom to be found in acceptance of our individual, genuine limitations. I use the word 'genuine' because I'm certainly not talking about giving up any idea of learning or improving in areas of weakness. Rather, I'm saying that when, like the prodigal son, we 'come to ourselves', the unalterable bedrock of what we are, we do better to offer that happily to God as our contribution to the body. There is no point in trying to be something we are not.

Sometimes it's necessary to be painfully vulnerable.

When I was first asked to contribute to the 9.15 'Pause for Thought' slot on BBC Radio 2, I was very keen but also very apprehensive. I was keen because this slot occurred in the middle of a very popular secular programme, and I felt reasonably confident that my style of speaking and writing would be appropriate to that particular audience.

The apprehension was caused by my awareness that I'm hopelessly defensive in the face of criticism. Negative comments erode my confidence so drastically that my performance is likely to become a pale, twittering, feeble version of what might have been possible. I'm not saying that I don't need to be criticized, but I am saying that I need to know that the person who is doing the criticizing values me or my work in the first place. Pathetic, isn't it? But that was my greatest worry when I first met Michael Wakelin (producer of 'Pause for Thought' at the time) in his London office.

As we sat and discussed my contribution to the programme, it suddenly occurred to me that I could try being totally vulnerable. It was uncomfortable—rather like showing your wooden leg to someone who has just suggested going for a run (I imagine).

'I might as well tell you,' I said, 'that the quality of the second programme I do will depend almost entirely on the way you react to the first.'

Michael, who is a charming fellow, looked a little taken aback. 'What do you mean?'

'Tell me it was wonderful.'

'Even if it's not?'

'Tell me it was wonderful whether it is or it isn't, and the next one almost certainly will be. If you pick the first one to bits I shall die inside, and they'll all be rubbish from then on.'

And that's what happened. After my first 'Pause for Thought' broadcast, Michael told me it was wonderful, I believed him by an act of the will, and the second one went very well.

The talents and abilities that I have are contained within a very fragile vessel, and I depend heavily on other people for help in developing and using them. A clear and uninflated view of our strengths, coupled with an equally realistic awareness of our weaknesses and limitations, cannot but strengthen the body of Christ.

You perhaps want to say to me that God might strengthen those weaknesses and reduce those fundamental limitations. Well, yes, he might, but that's his business, and, until he does, most of us have to work with what we've got, which boils down to ourselves—and each other.

I wonder what Michael did think of that first programme…

Pray with me

Father, when I come to the edge of me, I don't want to go walking foolishly forward like those cartoon characters who suddenly realize that they're walking on thin air and plummet to the ground, hundreds of feet below. I'll watch out for the signs. Help me to handle my own limits, Lord. Amen.

A voice from the darkness

At the sixth hour darkness came over the whole land until the ninth hour. And at the ninth hour Jesus cried out in a loud voice, *'Eloi, Eloi, lama sabachthani?'*—which means, 'My God, my God, why have you forsaken me?'

MARK 15:33–34

This passage offers us permission to speak truthfully from the darkness. Sometimes a sense of despair can be so profound that our prayers are full of doubts and questions. It is then, when we are most fearful and lost, that we should address God. That's what Jesus did.

Pray with me

On this particular day, I feel a failure.
What am I allowed to wonder, Father?
Am I allowed to wonder why you make it all so difficult?
Even as I say those words the guilt settles.
Perhaps it isn't really difficult at all.
Probably it's me that's difficult.
Probably, because of my background, and my temperament,
and my circumstances, it was always going to be difficult for me.
But what if that's just a cop-out?
What if I'm kidding myself?
What if, deep inside, I know that my own deliberate doing
and not doing has always made it difficult?
What if I'm one of those who has been called, but not chosen?
In that case it's not difficult—it's impossible.

What if you don't exist at all,
and death is a sudden stumble into silence?
(Can you let me know if you don't exist, by the way—
before Friday night, if it's all the same to you.)
There are moments, Father, when it's so easy,
so easy that I can't remember why it ever seemed so difficult.
Those moments pass—they're valuable—but they pass.
Have you noticed how, when those moments have gone,
I try to walk away, but I can't?
I think I shall follow you even if you don't exist.
Even if I'm not chosen.
Even if it goes on being difficult...
Are you still listening?
I'm sorry to have made a fuss,
it's just that, on this particular day, I feel a failure.
My feet and hands hurt,
And there's this pain in my side.

Gideon: a frightened man with a big task

Trouble without God

Again the Israelites did evil in the eyes of the Lord, and for seven years he gave them into the hands of the Midianites. Because the power of Midian was so oppressive, the Israelites prepared shelters for themselves in mountain clefts, caves and strongholds. Whenever the Israelites planted their crops, the Midianites, Amalekites and other eastern peoples invaded the country. They camped on the land and ruined the crops all the way to Gaza and did not spare a living thing for Israel, neither sheep nor cattle nor donkeys. They came up with their livestock and their tents like swarms of locusts. It was impossible to count the men and their camels; they invaded the land to ravage it. Midian so impoverished the Israelites that they cried out to the Lord for help. When the Israelites cried to the Lord because of Midian, he sent them a prophet, who said, 'This is what the Lord, the God of Israel, says: I brought you up out of Egypt, out of the land of slavery. I snatched you from the power of Egypt and from the hand of all your oppressors. I drove them from before you and gave you their land. I said to you, "I am the Lord your God; do not worship the gods of the Amorites, in whose land you live." But you have not listened to me.' The angel of the Lord came and sat down under the oak in Ophrah that belonged to Joash the Abiezrite, where his son Gideon was threshing wheat in a winepress to keep it from the Midianites.
JUDGES 6:1–11

It would be deeply irreverent of me to suggest that, in any way, we have God over a barrel, so I won't—but we have really. I know he can be very tough, and awesome in his power and strength, but he never gives up with us. He always wants us back, doesn't he? I don't consistently believe that wonderful truth in the front office of my head, but there's a heavy old file marked 'GOD LOVES YOU' locked away somewhere in a safe at the back. God himself put it there, and he kept the key, so I wouldn't be able to get rid of it even if I wanted to. I have wanted to sometimes, but he's never let me, thank goodness.

The same was true of God's people, the Israelites, right through the Old Testament. God never gave up. Now, as Gideon (one of my all-time favourite characters) is about to come on to the biblical stage, the nation has endured seven long years of miserable impoverishment at the hands of the powerful Midianites. What an existence! How very humiliating for a once-proud people to end up skulking in mountain caves or peering fearfully over stronghold walls, knowing that without God nothing will ever change, however hard they might work or fight.

These people had placed themselves in a prison of fear and oppression by their treacherous insistence on worshipping the false gods of the Amorites, but now they'd had enough. Like the prodigal son they came to themselves and cried to the one true God to come and save them yet again. In response, God spoke passionately to them about their disobedience, and then, because he had never stopped loving them, he devised a rescue plan and sent an angel to Ophrah to begin putting it into action.

I have placed myself into similar prisons over the years. I expect you have too. It's so easy to take the spiritual coin that God gives and spend it on things that he doesn't like and that are bad for us. Slowly, almost imperceptibly, our priorities change, as the false gods of this age ease their fatly contented selves on to the thrones of our lives.

The rot sets in. We become fearful and dissatisfied. There are too many enemies and we are too weak to resist. When we reach the bottom we begin to wonder if God can possibly still love us when we have been so far away for so long. Tentatively, we reach out towards him, hoping desperately that he will reach out towards us. Is it possible to move from fear to love? Gideon's story says that the answer to that question is 'Yes', but it also reminds us that God's rescue plans (including the most important one of all) almost invariably begin with something very small.

When the crunch comes

The angel of the Lord came and sat down under the oak in Ophrah that belonged to Joash the Abiezrite, where his son Gideon was threshing wheat in a winepress to keep it from the Midianites. When the angel of the Lord appeared to Gideon, he said, 'The Lord is with you, mighty warrior.' 'But sir,' Gideon replied, 'if the Lord is with us, why has all this happened to us? Where are all his wonders that our fathers told us about when they said, "Did not the Lord bring us up out of Egypt?" But now the Lord has abandoned us and put us into the hand of Midian.' The Lord turned to him and said, 'Go in the strength you have and save Israel out of Midian's hand. Am I not sending you?' 'But Lord,' Gideon asked, 'how can I save Israel? My clan is the weakest in Manasseh, and I am the least in my family.' The Lord answered, 'I will be with you, and you will strike down the Midianites as if they were but one man.'

JUDGES 6:11–16

I suppose angels get used to carrying out daft-sounding orders without question. This one must have been flabbergasted when he was told to go and address Gideon, of all people, as 'mighty warrior'. Gideon was singularly unimpressed, wasn't he? So would I have been, if I was the least important member of the least important family in the whole community, and some stranger with an advanced case of religious mania had solemnly announced that I was going to defeat the entire opposing army as if they were but one man. I'd have been on the phone to the local psychiatric facility insisting that they check numbers. And even if this *was* a messenger from the Lord, there was little recent evidence to suggest that God had either the power or the inclination to intervene as he had done in the past.

Gideon was going to take a lot of convincing, and I don't blame him. I know how it feels to be inwardly programmed for failure. I have felt small and useless. I've experienced the gnawing fear that when some awful crunch situation comes along I shall betray the people who rely on me most. Sometimes, usually in the middle of the night, I'm gripped by panic as my imagination pumps out grisly scenes in which members of my family die dreadful deaths while I stand uselessly aside, paralysed by fear and inadequacy. Curiously enough, although these fears are completely genuine, my response on the only occasion when I was tested in this way suggested that they might be quite unfounded. I'm aware that this will seem a very trivial incident, especially to those of my readers who have rescued people from burning buildings and wrestled with man-eating tigers, but it meant a lot to me.

Bridget and I had driven out one morning to a nearby village to visit a traditional tea-room whose beverages and cakes were, in our very humble opinion, the best in Sussex. We were particularly anxious that the trip should be a successful one because our last visit to this wonderful establishment had ended rather abruptly, when baby Katy threw up about as comprehensively as it can be done. The Plass children have always been generous with their undigested stomach contents, and Katy was no exception. She shared hers liberally and without favour between as many of our fellow customers as she could reach in one unconsciously artistic, spinning, centrifugal outpouring. The proprietors were very nice about it. They insisted that we should come back soon, but as we removed the husk of our little green daughter from the somewhat depressed, swamp-like atmosphere that she had created, we doubted that we would ever return.

Now, lured by base desire for more of that exceptional cake, we were back!

This time Katy was *not* sick, and we rejoiced over our total rehabilitation. We rejoiced a little too much. Or rather, I did. As we headed for the car, full of tea and cake, I did a small skip of celebration with Katy in my arms, and suddenly felt my balance slipping irretrievably away. I was about to fall flat on my face with Katy sandwiched between my considerable bulk and the hard tarmac of the car park. I didn't make any heroic decisions—there was no time for that. Katy not being hurt was all that mattered. Somehow I managed to twist my body in mid-topple, as it were, so that I landed on my back instead of my front. I was winded, and a bit bruised and scraped, but Katy was fine, if a little puzzled by our new game.

In the end it was the relationship that produced the spontaneous response, and of course it would have been exactly the same for any parent who loved his or her child.

I suspect that we would be well advised to concentrate on developing our closeness to Jesus, rather than dwelling gloomily on the probability that we will let him down, because it will be the reality or otherwise of that relationship that makes the difference when the crunch comes.

Pray with me

Father, it would be very foolish of us to pray for a crunch to come. Who needs unnecessary crunches? We know, though, that if we intend to follow you, anything can happen, and we want to be ready. When the testing time comes, may our love for you be greater than our fear. We would like to be so close to you that we are able not only to say, like Jesus at Gethsemane, 'Not my will be done, but yours', but to mean it as well. An awful lot of us are simply not in that place yet. Teach us individually how to strengthen the bond we have with you. We will try to talk more openly and more often with you. We will try to listen more to your voice. We will try to recognize you in the suffering folks around us. We will try to follow you into dark and dangerous places, and after that—it's up to you. Amen.

Physical fear

The same night the Lord said to him, 'Take the second bull from your father's herd, the one seven years old. Tear down your father's altar to Baal and cut down the Asherah pole beside it. Then build a proper kind of altar to the Lord your God on the top of this height. Using the wood of the Asherah pole that you cut down, offer the second bull as a burnt offering.' So Gideon took ten of his servants and did as the Lord told him. But because he was afraid of his family and the men of the town, he did it at night rather than in the daytime. In the morning when the men of the town got up, there was Baal's altar, demolished, with the Asherah pole beside it cut down and the second bull sacrificed on the newly built altar! They asked each other, 'Who did this?' When they carefully investigated, they were told, 'Gideon son of Joash did it.' The men of the town demanded of Joash, 'Bring out your son. He must die, because he has broken down Baal's altar and cut down the Asherah pole beside it.'
JUDGES 6:25–30

We don't talk much about fear of physical violence in the Church, do we? It's been a shadow in my life for as long as I can remember. Not that I have any problem with organized team violence. I enjoyed playing rugby when I was younger as much as anything else I've ever done. My anxiety is about deliberate, vicious hurting. Like Gideon, I would much rather perform acts of heroic defiance in the dark than openly risk retribution from those I have defied. Don't misunderstand me. I am not under the illusion that everyone else enjoys a healthy desire to be beaten to a pulp while I, rather strangely, react negatively to the proposition. What I'm talking about is a morbid preoccupation with the possibility of sudden, cataclysmically intrusive violence that crudely cancels out qualities of mind, spirit and emotion like a size-twelve boot squashing a snail.

I do not want my shell scrunched into my vulnerability.

I know it's a trite thing to say, but I have always been more frightened of the fear than the fact—always dreaded the humiliation more than the pain. This permanent and unpleasant inner shadow has been a feature of my life for so long that I doubt if I could trace its origin now.

One thing I do know, and I have touched on this in a previous book, is that my fear of violence in others is, at least in part, fuelled by a confused unwillingness to face the violence inside myself. Many of us (Christian or otherwise) are containing a lot of unresolved anger which tends to manifest itself as a sort of mild, ongoing, throbbing depression if it's never expressed or recognized. A very similar equation operates in the area of sexual jealousy, where all the lustful and unfaithful impulses of one, usually very insecure, partner are projected aggressively on to the other.

Do forgive me for this burst of amateur psychology, but these are real, often agonizing, problems in my life and the lives of people known to me.

My particular personal shadow caused me great distress when I was a young Christian in the 1960s. Everyone was reading about Richard Wurmbrand's experience of torture in the underground prisons of Romania. For fourteen years he refused to deny his faith, despite continual physical and mental suffering inflicted upon him by agents of a cruelly oppressive Communist regime.

FOURTEEN YEARS!

I seriously doubted that I would last four minutes, especially if they did anything to my teeth (did you see *Marathon Man*?). I just *knew* that I would emerge from that torture chamber a violently anti-Christian, deeply committed, proselytizing member of the Romanian Communist Party. I found it sufficiently fearful just walking through the mod-and-rocker-infested streets of my home town. All I could hope and pray was that the Christian population of Tunbridge Wells would never be faced with physical persecution. It seemed unlikely on the face of it...

The fear continued.

It continued throughout the years when I worked with teenagers in care, some of whom displayed extremely violent behaviour. Why on earth did I choose such work, given my particular weakness? I think the answer is that I would rather grapple voluntarily with the object of my fears than wait for the object of my fears to grapple unexpectedly with *me*.

The fear continued when I went to South Africa in the summer of 1993. On the evening before I went, I sat with my head in my hands at our kitchen table at home and said to God, 'I don't want to go. I'm frightened. What if I get shot or necklaced or beaten up or mugged or…' Temporarily running out of dismal possibilities at this point, I concluded with the words, 'And anyway, I've not got anything to say to the people out there—nothing useful, anyway.' There then began a familiar species of inner dialogue between myself and someone who, for the sake of argument, I will call God:

God: Why have they asked you to go to South Africa?
Me: They wrote and asked me if I'd come and cheer them up.
God: Well, what's wrong with that, then?
Me: *(Gracelessly)* Nothing, I suppose.
God: Well, go and do that as well as you can, then. And don't try to be clever. Don't tell them anything except what you've learned about me.
Me: All right, then. I will.

This completely imaginary dialogue with God made me feel a lot better—a pretty remarkable achievement for a completely imaginary dialogue with God, don't you think? I went to South Africa, and I think I did cheer some people up, but the fear was as bad as ever. On a few occasions I lay awake for most of the night, my mind constantly re-running scenes of violence and horror that I had been told of, or had seen on television news reports the previous evening. Other, more balanced, folk would have slept like babies. I couldn't. I was in a cold sweat. God did not take the fear away. I loved the people I met in that sad, beautiful, tumultuous land, but I almost kissed the tarmac when my return flight landed at Heathrow. (That is a very *Roman* sacrament, though, isn't it?)

The fear continues.

I don't know if God will ever perform divine surgery on me. I wish he *would* lift my weakness out by the roots. Perhaps, though, it will always be part of the cluster of thorns in my flesh (did Paul really only have *one* thorn?), and if he doesn't remove it, I hope that I continue to learn, as Gideon did with painful slowness, that God really can be trusted, however weak I am, and that obedience, and dependence of the right sort, are the things that will make me strong in the end.

And if you disagree with what I've said—don't hit me…

Pray with me

I've done it again, Lord. I've ended my comments with a flippancy. That's because I don't know how to write a scream. Anyone who shares this particular fear will understand about that scream. I've just told a friend from over the road that I was writing about fear of violence. He's a strong character, as you know, but something very deep relaxed in him as I spoke. He said, 'I have that fear as well.' And I knew it was the same. I could see it in his face. I was comforted by his honesty.

Should I pray to be released from this 40-year-old burden, Lord? I don't know if I can. The haversack has become a hump. I'm afraid that a lot of me would go with it if you removed it. I think we'll have to take it with us, but (hold on while I shut my eyes and grit my teeth) you're the boss. Amen.

What about me?

Gideon said to God, 'If you will save Israel by my hand as you have promised—look, I will place a wool fleece on the threshing-floor. If there is dew only on the fleece and all the ground is dry, then I will know that you will save Israel by my hand, as you said.' And that is what happened. Gideon rose early the next day; he squeezed the fleece and wrung out the dew—a bowlful of water. Then Gideon said to God, 'Do not be angry with me. Let me make just one more request. Allow me one more test with the fleece. This time make the fleece dry and the ground covered with dew.' That night God did so. Only the fleece was dry; all the ground was covered with dew.

JUDGES 6:36–40

A while ago, the tabloid newspapers were filled with transcriptions of telephone conversations involving members of the royal family and other well-known people. Here's one that the *Daily Mirror* missed. We can only hear one side of the conversation, and the speaker never actually identifies himself, although he's quite clearly a nonentity, but the person who appears to be on the other end of the phone—well, they don't come a lot more famous than him!

(Tape begins) Hello, is that God? … It is? Oh, good! I've had awful trouble getting through, you know… Yes, I kept getting this crackling on the line, then someone told me I'd got through to the wrong place, and… Oh, yes, very helpful, thanks, a real ang— a really helpful person… Sorry? … What can you do to help me? Well, a couple of small things. First of all, any chance of resolving the paradox of predestination and free will? Secondly, how about explaining why an omniscient, omnipotent, all-loving God created a world which contained

evil and was destined to fall? Thirdly, perhaps I could hear your reasons for allowing all the suffering that men and women have endured since the beginning of time. Oh, and fourthly, you might tell me why there's such a delay on the Porsche… You think what, God? … You think those questions will take so long to answer that I'd better join you up there *now* so that you can get started? Ha! ha! Good one, God! You knew I was joking really, didn't you? Not that I don't want to be with you, you understand. Of course I do. Really looking forward to it—in a way…

Was there what? … Was there something serious I wanted to say? Well, yes, there was actually. I've just been reading the story of Gideon, and I must say, God, it is one of my favourite bits in the Bible. Really inspired… no, I didn't mean that—of course it is. It's *all* inspired, God. No, I just meant that it's such a good story… sorry, yes, such a good historical account —that's what I meant to say… What? … Yes, of course there are lots of other good bits… Song of Solomon? Yes, excellent and very moving poetry, God, but Gideon is… yes… yes… yes, I do think Revelation has all the haunting drama of a vast uncharted mountain range offering jagged defiance to a brooding, storm-filled sky. Very nicely put, God. You're very creative, you know… oh, don't mention it, thank you very much for—well, for everything I suppose, really. Err, just quickly about Gideon, God. Look, I don't want to sound as if I'm complaining, but… What? … You think I sound as if I am about to complain. Well, I suppose I am really. It's just that I don't really understand why you were so patient with Gideon. I mean, first of all he wanted proof that you were *pleased* with him (excuse me while I throw up), so you organized a little barbie on a rock for him so that he'd know you were *pleased* with him. Then, when he had all this proof that you were pleased with him, he lost his bottle, didn't he? … No, let me just finish, God. Then, when you wanted him to smash that idol and pull down his old man's symbol of Asherah, whoever she might be when she's at home, he did it in the middle of the *night*, God! Were you cross? No! Did his father tell him off? No! Did poor little Gideon gain any confidence from all this evidence that you were *pleased* with him! Of course not. He had you up two nights running, fussing and fiddling about with fleeces and grass and dew, trying to remember what was supposed to be wet and what was supposed to be dry, while he snored like a pig all night, just so that the poor fragile little chap could be *absolutely, definitely, one hundred per cent sure* that you were *pleased* with him! ...

What am I trying to say? Nothing really... Am I what? ... Jealous? Don't make me laugh! How could I be jealous of a lily-livered, chicken-hearted, ungrateful, spineless son of an idol-worshipper like Gideon? Yes, I *am* jealous! Of course I'm jealous. When did I ever get all that proof and encouragement and molly-coddling from you? Answer—never! Not so much as a fried prawn. Sometimes I'm afraid you just don't care about me—well, *say* something... *(Tape ends)*

Pray with me

Why don't you communicate as clearly with us as you did with Gideon, Lord? Yes, I did hear that great angelic gasp echoing through heaven, and they're quite right, of course. Sometimes you do communicate very directly nowadays—you have with me once or twice—but you know what I mean. Do you know what I mean? I'll tell you what I mean.

Gideon had a big job to do, so he needed all the reassurance he could get, but we could do with a bit of that as well, Lord. We keep saying things to each other like, 'God is holding out his hand to offer us guidance and love and help in every part of our lives. All we've got to do is take it.' And we all nod ruefully, and say, 'Yes, how true that is.' But it isn't like that, Lord. Whatever anyone says—it isn't like that. Many of us are in desperate need of you, but can't seem to find you.

Here is my prayer for today, Father. Show each of us what stands in the way of real contact with you. Be tough. If it's impurity or anger or disobedience—whatever it is, show us. Lead us into a place where we can know the kind of love and reassurance that upheld Gideon.

Thank you. Amen.

God in action

Early in the morning, Jerub-Baal (that is, Gideon) and all his men camped at the spring of Harod. The camp of Midian was north of them in the valley near the hill of Moreh. The Lord said to Gideon, 'You have too many men for me to deliver Midian into their hands. In order that Israel may not boast against me that her own strength has saved her, announce now to the people, "Anyone who trembles with fear may turn back and leave Mount Gilead."' So twenty-two thousand men left, while ten thousand remained. But the Lord said to Gideon, 'There are still too many men. Take them down to the water, and I will sift them out for you there. If I say, "This one shall go with you," he shall go; but if I say, "This one shall not go with you," he shall not go.' So Gideon took the men down to the water. There the Lord told him, 'Separate those who lap the water with their tongues like a dog from those who kneel down to drink.' Three hundred men lapped with their hands to their mouths. All the rest got down on their knees to drink. The Lord said to Gideon, 'With the three hundred men who lapped I will save you and give the Midianites into your hands. Let all the other men go, each to his own place.' So Gideon sent the rest of the Israelites to their tents but kept the three hundred, who took over the provisions and trumpets of the others.

JUDGES 7:1–8

God: Gideon, I've been thinking.

Gideon: *(Nervously)* Mmmm?

God: You're not frightened of the Midianites, are you? I mean, they're not very clever, are they?

Gideon: No, thick as locusts, I've heard. Why?

God: Well, we wouldn't want anyone to start boasting that Israel has saved herself, would we?

Gideon: No, heaven forb— No, of course not.

God: So I've had an idea.

Gideon: (*Uneasily*) Oh, good. (*Pause*) What is it?

God: Well, I thought we could cut the army down a bit.

Gideon: (*Thoughtfully*) Yeees, not such a bad idea. Wouldn't do any harm to lose the elderly and the sick, and maybe the very young. That should lose a couple of hundr—

God: I was thinking you could announce that anyone who's frightened doesn't have to fight.

Gideon: Oh dear.

God: (*Cheerfully*) That should make a difference, shouldn't it?

Gideon: (*Hollowly*) Oh, yes. That should make a difference.

God: Right! Off you go and tell them, then.

Gideon: Look, I'll just go and get my fleece and—

God: No, no. No more fleeces. Just go and tell them. I'll wait here. OK?

Gideon: (*Numbly*) OK.
          (*Gideon exits slowly. God whistles 'Fight the good fight' as he waits. After a minute or so a huge cheer is heard outside. Gideon re-enters, a pale shadow of the pale shadow of himself that he was before he went out.*)

God: How did it go?

Gideon: (*Faintly*) Fine.

God: Lose many?

Gideon: Twenty-two thousand. (*Suddenly panic-stricken*) Twenty-two thousand of them have gone home, God! Are you sure that was such a good idea? You're not seriously suggesting that I take on the Midianites with ten thousand men, are you? You're not, are you? (*Pause*) You are, aren't you?

God: (*He laughs*) Attack the Midianites with an army of ten thousand men? Of course not!

Gideon: (*He laughs too*) Well, thank goodness for—

God: No, that's far too many.
          (*Pause*)

Gideon: I'll get my fleece—

God:	No, listen—I've got a really good idea for cutting the army down even more.
Gideon:	*(Morosely)* Oh, what's that, then? Anyone who's never wanted to be boiled in oil can go home? That should leave us with a very small group of complete loonies.
God:	No, this is a really interesting one. Take all ten thousand of the ones who are left down to the water and watch how they drink.
Gideon:	Down to the water?
God:	Yep!
Gideon:	Watch how they drink?
God:	Yep!
Gideon:	God?
God:	Mmmm?
Gideon:	There's quite a move to cart me off to the funny-farm as it is, after my last great tactical ploy. Now you're suggesting I go and stand on that hill again, and announce that I want all ten thousand of them to march down to the water so that I can watch them drink. They might wonder why I want them to do that, God. I know I'm going to wish I hadn't asked this question, but—*why would* I want to make them do something like that?
God:	Ah, well, you see, all the ones who kneel down and drink straight from the river, we'll get rid of, right? And we'll keep all the ones who lap from their hands.
Gideon:	*(Slightly hysterical)* Of course! Silly me! Of course that's what we'll do! I'll go and do it now.
	(Later)
God:	How's it going?
Gideon:	*(Dully)* Three hundred left. Tents and provisions for thirty-two thousand being shared by three hundred dentally handy-lapped men. God?
God:	Yes?
Gideon:	I'm frightened.
God:	Of course you are! But I've had this really, really good idea.

Gideon: Oh, you haven't, have you?

God: Yes, what you do is, you go down to the Midianite camp tonight in disguise, and while you're there...

Pray with me

Father, when you really take hold of our lives, the speed and energy with which you work can be quite bewildering. Once or twice, when you've taken a situation I'm involved in by the scruff of the neck, I've found myself almost wanting to back out. We yearn so much to be actively working with and for you, but the reality is daunting, to say the least. Help us, please, to recognize the qualities of humour, fondness and excited creativity that actually characterize much of your dealings with men and women.

We have many false gods in this age, but we have to confess that one of the most damaging ones of all is the God who cannot smile, never really does anything, and doesn't like us.

Are you laughing at me? Amen.

Into the enemy camp

During that night the Lord said to Gideon, 'Get up, go down against the camp, because I am going to give it into your hands. If you are afraid to attack, go down to the camp with your servant Purah and listen to what they are saying. Afterwards, you will be encouraged to attack the camp.' So he and Purah his servant went down to the outposts of the camp. The Midianites, the Amelekites and all the other eastern peoples had settled in the valley, thick as locusts. Their camels could no more be counted than the sand on the seashore. Gideon arrived just as a man was telling a friend his dream. 'I had a dream,' he was saying. 'A round loaf of barley bread came tumbling into the Midianite camp. It struck the tent with such force that the tent overturned and collapsed.' His friend responded, 'This can be nothing other than the sword of Gideon son of Joash, the Israelite. God has given the Midianites and the whole camp into his hands.' When Gideon heard the dream and its interpretation, he worshipped God. He returned to the camp of Israel and called out, 'Get up! The Lord has given the Midianite camp into your hands.'

JUDGES 7:9–15

The other day, in Southampton, my taxi driver, a man in his early 60s, was forced to stop for a minute while a jam of vehicles sorted itself out. A youngish, tough-looking character who was doing something to his parked car on the other side of the road waved and called out loudly in our direction.

'Loady, loady, loady!' he shouted jovially.

My driver responded to this odd communication as if it was the most hilarious joke he'd ever heard. Winding his window right down, he leaned out, saluted the other man enthusiastically with a stiff raised arm, and yelled energetically back across the road:

'Loady, loady, loady!'

Both men were almost convulsed with matey, back-slapping laughter as my taxi pulled away, but I was puzzled. Why would two normal men shout something like 'Loady, loady, loady!' at each other? I mean—why? Not for the first time I felt excluded from this world of strangely coded bonhomie. All through my life I seemed to have heard working men exchanging obscure, tribal cries, and then guffawing helplessly (and quite inexplicably, as far as I was concerned). I had never had the temerity to enquire about the meaning of these mystical expressions. I just felt left out and goofily middle-class.

As my taxi sped along towards the station, a staggeringly novel idea formed in my perplexed mind. Why should I not—just for once—find out what these two fellows had been talking about? Nervously, I opened my mouth, and entered the camp to which I did not belong, all too ready to retreat when defeat and humiliation overwhelmed me.

'Just now,' I said, 'when we had to stop, that guy on the other side of the road shouted something at you.'

'Yeah, that's right.'

'He shouted "Loady, loady, loady", didn't he?'

'Yeah, that's right.'

'And you shouted "Loady, loady, loady" back, didn't you?'

'Back—yeah, that's right.'

'And then you both laughed, right?'

'Both laughed, yeah, that's right, yeah.'

I cleared my throat before asking the next, crucial question, mentally preparing myself for the scornful amazement with which he would receive the news that such ignorance was possible.

'I just wondered—what does "Loady, loady, loady" actually mean?'

'Dunno.'

'You don't know?'

'Ain't got the faintest, mate.'

For a few seconds I was bereft of words. He didn't know! He didn't know! How could he *not* know? Was the world really inhabited by lunatics who shouted 'Loady, loady, loady!' at each other for no reason at all, and then fell about laughing?

'But look,' I said, almost pleadingly, 'after he'd said it, you said it, and then you and him laughed as if you both knew what you were talking about, and…'

'Ah, well, 'e beats up taxi drivers, see?'

'He beats up—'

'Beat up one of our blokes last week. Gets drunk, see. Scumbag when 'e's drunk, that bloke. Nasty piece o' work, 'e is. When a bloke like that says "Loady, loady, loady" you don't ask 'im what 'e's on about. You just say "Loady, loady, loady" back, doncher?'

'Will he get done for beating up your—friend?'

'Too right! It was me reported 'im. None of the others was goin' to, but I said you can't let people like 'im get away with it, so I reported 'im. I expect when 'e finds out it was me 'e'll come lookin' for *me* an' all. Gotta do what's right though, aincher?'

'What do you think the courts will give him?' My companion pondered for a moment, then smiled grimly.

'I 'ope,' he said, 'they give 'im Loady, loady, loady…'

'So what has all this got to do with Gideon creeping into the camp of the Midianites?' I seem to hear you say. Well, I suppose it's just that my complete misreading of the 'Loady, loady, loady' incident was caused by an ugly amalgam of prejudices, fears and misconceptions about something that I foolishly and fearfully thought of as *the way working men relate to each other*. On this rare occasion when, by asking my question, I actually entered the camp of those who threatened me, I discovered that there were very complex issues at stake, and that those two men who had seemed to be identical stones in a wall that excluded me, could not, in fact, have been more different.

It might be useful to reflect that the road to freedom from fear will sometimes involve an expedition into the centre of the very thing that threatens us. In that place we may, like Gideon, learn a new truth that will fill us with hope. And if anyone out there knows what 'Loady, loady, loady!' means, please let me know.

Pray with me

What do you think of your flabby old Church, Lord? I know you love and cherish it, but you must get so fed up with our reluctance to tread unknown or threatening paths because we're frightened of people or situations that are alien to us. I'm afraid that if Jesus came back in the flesh today he wouldn't be much more popular in the Church than he was two thousand years ago. Would I follow him to the rough pubs and the gay clubs if he asked me to go? I don't know, Lord. I just don't know.

We pray for wisdom and courage—wisdom to know when the time has come to step into the enemy camp, and Holy Spirit courage to enable us to do it. Forgive our timidity, Lord. Amen.

P.S. I'm not sure if I want you to answer this prayer.

Into battle

Dividing the three hundred men into three companies, he placed trumpets and empty jars in the hands of all of them, with torches inside. 'Watch me,' he told them. 'Follow my lead. When I get to the edge of the camp, do exactly as I do. When I and all who are with me blow our trumpets, then from all around the camp blow yours and shout, "For the Lord and for Gideon."' Gideon and the hundred men with him reached the edge of the camp at the beginning of the middle watch, just after they had changed the guard. They blew their trumpets and broke the jars that were in their hands. The three companies blew the trumpets and smashed the jars. Grasping the torches in their left hands and holding in their right hands the trumpets they were to blow, they shouted, 'A sword for the Lord and for Gideon!' While each man held his position around the camp, all the Midianites ran, crying out as they fled. When the three hundred trumpets sounded, the Lord caused the men throughout the camp to turn on each other with their swords.

JUDGES 7:16–22

In the list of questions that I'm going to ask God when I get to heaven (you should see the list he's got for me), number 31,974 goes as follows: 'Why do your dealings with men involve such a strange mixture of supernatural intervention and practical common sense?'

This attack of Gideon's is a very good example. As we've seen, God was very concerned that the Israelites should not end up patting themselves on the back after the Midianites were defeated. It was a divine initiative using a very reluctant leader who had to be 'fleeced' into believing that he really was going to be supported.

But all that business of cutting down the army wasn't just heavenly vanity. First of all, the 'tremblers' were removed. That left Gideon with ten thousand men who were either very brave or very stupid. The

70

next culling exercise removed the stupid ones. The men who knelt and drank straight from the water were clearly less aware and alert than those who, because they lapped from their hands in an upright position, would see, and have a chance of withstanding, a surprise attack.

The Israelite force was reduced to a mere three hundred, but they must have been a very select body of fighting men. As Gideon organized the distribution of jars, torches and trumpets (sounds like a Salvation Army open-air evening street mission, doesn't it?) in preparation for the execution of this startlingly creative battle plan, he knew that he had the best. Not the most—but the best.

What an appalling shock for the sleeping Midianites to be suddenly surrounded by sound and light where there had been only silence and darkness. Morale was already low in the enemy camp, as Gideon's secret mission had revealed. No wonder the enemy soldiers turned their swords on each other, confused and panic-stricken by an attack that seemed to be all around them and in their very midst.

Gideon had done it. God must have been exhausted.

The story of Gideon suggests some very interesting and perhaps significant principles:

1. It is God who initiates the battles we shall be involved in, not us. The Church wastes an awful lot of time with things that 'seem like a good idea'.
2. God chooses weak and fearful people for the big tasks. We may find that encouraging or terrifying—or both.
3. The credit has to go to God, not to the Church of England, nor the Evangelical Alliance, nor Gideon, nor Adrian Plass. God will shake down individuals and institutions until they are seen to be the most pure and basic unit capable of carrying out a divine commission.
4. God is more practical than we are. The ways in which he prepares us may seem strange at times, but the result will be something that *works* in the real world. Most of the miracles occur in the process that brings us to a belief that God will be there when we most need him.
5. The battle will be won.

Take heart, my fellow fearful ones. If Gideon could do it, then so can we—can't we?

Pray with me

Father, we would like to respond to the lessons that you've taught us through this extraordinary story.

Show us what you're doing, and we'll join in. Don't let us get caught up in weird and wonderful schemes that you don't approve of.

You choose weak and fearful people to carry out your plans. Hey—we qualify for once!

Give us the patience to accept the training and the 'shaking down' that will make us ready for the job. Remind us that the credit goes to you.

Thank you for the potent blend of supernatural and practical that distinguishes your way of working from the world's way.

We know the war is already won, Lord, but give us a place in the last battle. We want to be with you when you win. Amen.

Disciples: a motley crew

Conjuring or compassion?

When they came to the crowd, a man approached Jesus and knelt before him. 'Lord, have mercy on my son,' he said. 'He has seizures and is suffering greatly. He often falls into the fire or into the water. I brought him to your disciples, but they could not heal him.' 'O unbelieving and perverse generation,' Jesus replied, 'how long shall I stay with you? How long shall I put up with you? Bring the boy here to me.' Jesus rebuked the demon, and it came out of the boy, and he was healed from that moment.

MATTHEW 17:14–18

I wonder if it was the passion in this heartbroken father that had taken the wind out of the disciples' sails. I bet they'd been swanning around like blow-wave evangelists, don't you? Can you picture them casting out a devil here, healing a chronic sickness there—distributing miraculous largesse like divine Lords of the Manor? What an experience, to have the power and authority to change lives so suddenly and so effectively. For a while it must have been so easy. Every one a winner. Perhaps they got a bit carried away with the 'Paul Daniels' aspect of ministry.

Then, along comes this desperate parent, full of urgent suffering and unimpressed by anyone's power, except in so far as it might be helpful to his beloved son. Did the raw need of this particular supplicant knock away the foundations of faith that had been laid in the disciples as they walked and talked with their master?

Supposing it didn't work this time?

What if the boy got worse instead of better?

How would this man cope if his final hopes were dashed?

What would the 'audience' say if the great healers failed?

Conjectural, perhaps, but this particular scenario has been repeated, with cultural variations, throughout the two thousand years since Jesus' disciples first blew it. Ministry without compassion is still very much with us today, and it is no less likely to fail when confronted by stark, uncompromising need. A lot of people who speak with total assurance from the safety of platforms are quite lost when confronted by those annoying individuals who have believed what they were told, and are now asking very simply for some of the practical assistance that was preached so boldly and theoretically. I'm quite sure that some of the work I've done has been diluted in effectiveness by my cowardice when it comes to offering direct prayer or ministry to those who have taken seriously something I've said.

I blush, even as I write.

Pray with me

Father, I see so much failure in Christian ministry, and we hardly ever talk about it. Does it make you very sad, or very angry, or both, when people lose their courage like me, or else try to counterfeit the power of the Holy Spirit to do religious conjuring tricks? All the funny voices, and the strange gestures and expressions, and the excuses and rationalizations when it 'doesn't work'—what are we to make of all that, Lord?

Inhabit us with your true care, Jesus. Make us bold and honest in your name. Live your compassion through our hands and our lives. No more games, eh? No more games that fail suffering people. We step aside, Lord. Amen.

Faith works, not works

Then the disciples came to Jesus in private and asked, 'Why couldn't we drive it out?' He replied, 'Because you have so little faith. I tell you the truth, if you have faith as small as a mustard seed, you can say to this mountain, "Move from here to there" and it will move. Nothing will be impossible for you.'

MATTHEW 17:19–21

Did the disciples think that Jesus would point out some trifling deficiency in their healing technique—something they could change next time? Why do we cling to the belief that if we change in some way, then God will start to work? Do these words find an echo in you?

Once I've cleaned this house up properly,
I honestly think I'll get somewhere.
Once I've pulled out every single piece of furniture and used
an abrasive cloth with strong stuff on it,
I think I shall come to grips with the rest of my life.
Once I've put everything into separate piles, each containing
the same sort of thing (if you know what I mean)
I think I'll manage.
Once I've written a list that includes absolutely everything,
I think the whole business will seem very much clearer.
Once I've had time to work slowly from one item to another,
I'm sure things will change.
Once I've eaten sensibly for more than a week and a half,
Once I've sorted out the things that are my fault,
Once I've sorted out the things that are not my fault,
Once I've spent a little more time reading useful books,
Being with people I like,

Going to pottery classes,
Getting out into the air,
Making bread,
Drinking less,
Drinking more,
Going to the theatre,
Adopting a Third-World child,
Eating free-range eggs,
And writing long letters,
Once I've pulled every single piece of furniture right out,
And cleaned this house up properly,
Once I've become somebody else…
I honestly think I'll get somewhere.

Pray with me

I suppose it's a good thing really, Father, that not too many of us have got faith the size of a mustard seed. Can you imagine all the vast natural objects of the world sliding around crazily as irresponsible Christians exercise their faith as though they're playing a cosmic computer game? Or perhaps faith and maturity go together automatically—no, perhaps not…

Seriously though, Lord, when we have accepted that we're never going to be perfect enough to do it all on our own, where does this amazing faith that you mention come from? We don't see many people moving mountains (or small rocks for that matter) nowadays. If it's a gift from you, and I think the Bible says it is, then we'd like to have it, please. If it comes from hearing your voice clearly, then unblock our ears. If we need to grow up a bit before we can be trusted with such a powerful secret weapon, then show us the pathways to maturity. Give us faith, even if it's only a fiftieth of the size of a mustard seed. Amen.

Sin, sifting and salvation

'Simon, Simon, Satan has asked to sift you as wheat. But I have prayed for you, Simon, that your faith may not fail. And when you have turned back, strengthen your brothers.' But he replied, 'Lord, I am ready to go with you to prison and to death.' Jesus answered, 'I tell you, Peter, before the cock crows today, you will deny three times that you know me.'
LUKE 22:31–34

Jesus must have felt such love for this fierce, strong, weak child of a disciple. In the pre-Pentecost phase Peter was still very much at the mercy of his own complex personality. Presumably he was capable of failing completely. We can only guess, but perhaps the prayers of his Master swung the balance when he had to decide whether to stay with the other disciples after the denials and the crucifixion, or to go somewhere far away from all the dark memories. What a tragedy if he had taken the latter course, and not been with the others when Jesus made his second appearance after rising from the dead. Satan certainly did sift Simon Peter, but the love and prayers of Jesus overcame the power of evil, and the chaos in this particular human being.

I meet a lot of people who fear the outcome of being sifted. It conjures up a very unpleasant picture—the devil, with a sneering grin on his face, picking contemptuously through the rubbish of our lives, every now and then pulling out some little thing that we might have thought worthwhile and holding it up to be ridiculed by the hosts of hell. Peter had really believed that he would support his Master to the end, but, as we have already seen, when it became clear that support would have to be on Jesus' terms, he didn't even have the courage to admit that he knew the sad-eyed Son of God.

And that, if we're honest, is the thing many of us fear most. We may not be committing huge, scarlet sins, but we are dismally aware of our capacity for sinking to the bottom of our flawed personalities. We can end up feeling too pinched and shabby and mean and trivial in our tedious little wrongdoings even to contemplate contact with God. It is very difficult to recover from this anti-climactic sense of failure.

I drank too much again last night.

I said I'd pray for someone and I didn't, then I said I had.

I won an argument with my husband by cheating.

I spent much of the Bible study dreaming about the girl opposite.

I've still got the day before yesterday's list of things that had to be done by yesterday and I haven't done any of them, and now I'll have to add on today's list of things that have to be done by tomorrow, and I haven't got time to do any of them, so the list will get longer and longer and longer as my life goes on and there won't be room for anything in my house except my list…

Such dank ordinariness.

Let's be positive. The Bible is a very dramatic book, but it's about very ordinary people. Jesus knew, when he took on characters like Peter, that he didn't have a team of superheroes under his leadership. He knew that the process of teaching and training and preparing them for the coming of the Holy Spirit after his death was going to be a tough, granular business. We Christians are not living in a Cecil B. De Mille Bible epic. We are grappling with true reality and God knows that.

Jesus loved Peter, weaknesses and all. He loves us in the same way.

Jesus prayed for Peter, that he would survive the process of being sifted. He prays for us in heaven at this very moment, passionately beseeching his Father to look at his death on the cross rather than at our ordinary or extraordinary sins.

Pray with me

Everything feels very sort of ordinary sometimes, Jesus. I don't feel as if I could ever fit into something like the book of Revelation with my spindly little sins and my undercooked virtues. I feel so pathetic a lot of the time, and I suspect that the devil would just get bored if he were to sift through me. Do you really find it worthwhile to pray for me to your Father? I find that very encouraging at the moment, and I want to thank you for being so much on my side. It makes me feel a little tearful to think of you battling away on my behalf like that. Thank you, Jesus. Amen.

I did it his way

Then Jesus told them, 'This very night you will all fall away on account of me, for it is written, "I will strike the shepherd, and the sheep of the flock will be scattered." But after I have risen, I will go ahead of you into Galilee.' Peter replied, 'Even if all fall away on account of you, I never will.' 'I tell you the truth,' Jesus answered, 'this very night, before the cock crows, you will disown me three times.' But Peter declared, 'Even if I have to die with you, I will never disown you.' And all the other disciples said the same.

MATTHEW 26:31–35

We get a bit patronizing about old Peter, don't we? He's often portrayed as a personality we can identify with, a sort of thick but amiable teddy-bear type, full of weaknesses that are just like ours. In fact, he was a jolly sight more courageous than most of us would have been. When he said he was willing to die with his Master, he meant exactly that, and when the arresting force came for Jesus in the garden he proved it by drawing his sword and going for the nearest human target.

There is a sign on the walls outside many South African houses that says: *Immediate Armed Response*. During my first visit to the city of Johannesburg I asked what this aggressive message meant. I was told that because of the increasing frequency of burglaries and violence there was a growing number of firms who specialized in domestic protection. Armed trucks patrolled constantly, ready to respond at a moment's notice to alarm calls from clients. (A rather alarming additional piece of information claimed that some of these firms were not above sending small boys out to throw stones through householders' windows in order to stimulate trade!)

Peter was genuinely ready to produce an immediate armed

response of his own, because he was certainly not a coward in the worldly sense. But (and here is something most of us can identify with), he wanted to choose the context within which he would serve. After Jesus had not only ruled out the option of force, but actually *healed* the first and only enemy casualty, Peter was unwilling or unable to move from his personal agenda of physical resistance into the bewildering context of voluntary captivity. It would be as if those South African householders, on encountering burglars, were flatly to refuse help from the security firm, and insist on presenting the intruders with everything that they wanted.

Why on earth, Peter must have puzzled wildly at that moment, if Jesus really had easy access to twelve legions of angels, didn't he whistle them up?

Peter wasn't into divine foolishness at that stage.

It's so easy to promise all sorts of things to God and other people on the assumption that we'll be allowed to carry out those promises using the strengths and techniques and approaches that are specially ours. But it's never been as simple as that. God chooses the weapons and the ways, while we stagger reluctantly towards unconditional obedience.

One of the most frightening things about following Jesus is his requirement that we abandon responsibility for deciding how we will help him. Some very strong people are going to feel extremely weak. Tough, isn't it?

Pray with me

Lord, sometimes I have run away. Help me to keep my mouth shut about what I'm going to do for you until I know what I'm talking about. I know what I think I can do, but I want to be able to abandon my own agenda in favour of yours, and it's not easy.

Perhaps I'm doing more than you want from me at the moment. Please stop me. I'm wasting my time.

Perhaps I have some talent that seems to indicate such a plain path for the future that I'm not even considering anything else. Stop me if I've got blinkered, Lord. I'm wasting my time.

Maybe I've got so involved in planning all sorts of things on your behalf that I've stopped asking you if we're on the same road. Pull me up, Lord. I'm wasting my time.

Perhaps I've known for longer than I care to admit that the time has come to tell the truth. Help me not to waste any more time, Lord. Amen.

Good enough?

Now Peter was sitting out in the courtyard, and a servant girl came to him. 'You also were with Jesus of Galilee,' she said. But he denied it before them all. 'I don't know what you're talking about,' he said. Then he went out to the gateway, where another girl saw him and said to the people there, 'This fellow was with Jesus of Nazareth.' He denied it again, with an oath: 'I don't know the man!' After a little while, those standing there went up to Peter and said, 'Surely you are one of them, for your accent gives you away.' Then he began to call down curses on himself and he swore to them, 'I don't know the man!' Immediately a cock crowed. Then Peter remembered the word Jesus had spoken: 'Before the cock crows, you will disown me three times.' And he went outside and wept bitterly.

MATTHEW 26:69–75

I wept a little just now, when I read this passage for the umpteenth time. There were two reasons for the tears.

First, I was suddenly, wearily conscious of how many times I have denied Jesus since I responded to the story of the thief on the cross 28 years ago. In my own way I have observed from outer courtyards, retreated to porches, and wildly protested my non-involvement. This isn't surprising because I'm a very flawed human being, and that leads to the second reason for my tears.

I know now that the only thing I can offer God is myself, and he will gladly, smilingly welcome that self, but the child in me wanted so much to be *good enough*. I find it painfully difficult to accept that God called me in the full knowledge that I was bound to let him down and betray him at one time or another. How hard it is for people as proud as many of us are to be *known* to such a depth—to feel all our human defences, tricks and pretences being gradually stripped away, and to see the naked poverty that is our real condition. We mourn for our spurious human dignity even as we plead for it to be removed.

Separated by two thousand years and nothing at all, Peter and I, and many others, go out and weep bitterly together because we fail our Master and because he always knew that we would.

Come and meet Jesus

You are standing alone outside the door of a huge, dark old traditional church, somewhere in the depths of East Anglia. It is a weekday evening in late autumn. Dusk has fallen and it seems most unlikely that the church will have been left unlocked and vulnerable in such a desolate area. But a cold November wind is whistling through the poorly tended graveyard, so you decide it might be worth a try. To your surprise, both the outer and inner doors are unlocked, and you are able to pass easily, if rather timidly, to the interior of the building, shutting the heavy old door carefully behind you as you go. You are a little worried that someone may be doing something important inside. They might be annoyed by your intrusion.

There is someone there. Behind the altar rail, far away at the opposite end of the church, lit by a large candle on either side of him, a man is facing you—waiting quietly. Somehow you know it's Jesus, and that he wants to give communion to you with his own hands. You very nearly give in to the temptation to escape. It would be so easy to pull the studded oak door open and run through the porch into the cold night. Instead, you walk towards the altar with your head bowed, frightened to meet his steady gaze because—because. You kneel at the rail and wait, still looking at the floor. A moment later you become aware that he has knelt too. His hand is gently lifting your chin until you can't help looking straight into his eyes. He speaks softly to you.

What does he say?

That's me all over...

On the evening of that first day of the week, when the disciples were together, with the doors locked for fear of the Jews, Jesus came and stood among them and said, 'Peace be with you!' After he said this, he showed them his hands and side. The disciples were overjoyed when they saw the Lord. Again Jesus said, 'Peace be with you! As the Father has sent me, I am sending you.' And with that he breathed on them and said, 'Receive the Holy Spirit. If you forgive anyone his sins, they are forgiven; if you do not forgive them, they are not forgiven.' Now Thomas (called Didymus), one of the Twelve, was not with the disciples when Jesus came. So the other disciples told him, 'We have seen the Lord!' But he said to them, 'Unless I see the nail marks in his hands and put my finger where the nails were, and put my hand into his side, I will not believe it.'

John 20:19–25

I've always had a soft spot for old Thomas, but it does seem reasonable to assume that he was *meant* to be with the others in this locked house (keen cricketers will be aware that the Twelfth Man must be physically present for all important fixtures). He was one of Jesus' original followers—of course he was supposed to be there when that joy-filled, astonished band of disciples felt the Spirit breathed upon them, and had the power of spiritual life and death placed into their hands.

Why was he missing? We don't know for certain, but we can guess, from the little we know of Thomas, that his absence might well have been due to some typically negative attitude to (on this occasion) the idea of gathering together.

Honest but pig-headed, he failed. He wasn't there when Jesus came. He thought he *knew*, but he didn't.

How strange it would be for Thomas to come back to earth two millennia after the events recorded here, to find that his name is permanently associated with the concept of 'doubt'. I hope it doesn't happen to me. Can you imagine the gossip in church circles two thousand years from now?

'Well, he's all right really—a bit of an Irritable Adrian, if you know what I mean.'

Pray with me

We feel quite nervous about stepping aside from what we are, don't we, Father? Why do we let these dominating personality traits lead us by the nose? How interesting it would be to see how our lives might change if we didn't automatically doubt, or get irritable, or look for problems, or become defensive, or revert to flippancy, or whatever our particular speciality happens to be. I think, Father, that the quickest way to find out what my responsive habits are is to ask my family, but I have an awful feeling that they'd tell me. In any case, I think I know! Lord, I don't want to be trapped by these silly things. Help me to find enough courage to experiment with leaving them out. Amen.

A motley crew

A week later his disciples were in the house again, and Thomas was with them. Though the doors were locked, Jesus came and stood among them and said, 'Peace be with you!' Then he said to Thomas, 'Put your finger here; see my hands. Reach out your hand and put it into my side. Stop doubting and believe.' Thomas said to him, 'My Lord and my God!' Then Jesus told him, 'Because you have seen me, you have believed; blessed are those who have not seen and yet have believed.'

JOHN 20:26–29

Forgive me, but I feel a bit of symbolism coming on (it tends to get worse when the weather turns). It was one sentence in this passage that did it. 'Though the doors were locked, Jesus came and stood among them and said, "Peace be with you!"'

Wasn't it nice of Jesus to give his doubting disciple a second chance, despite the fact that Thomas had shut his own inner doors of trust? And I really do believe that the same principle holds good today, although I don't think we are practised enough in allowing it to affect our lives.

Consider this for a moment.

Earlier in John's Gospel we hear Jesus telling his sorrowful friends that it will be *better* for them if he goes, because then the Holy Spirit can come. Better? Is he joking? What on earth is he talking about? What could possibly be better than having Jesus himself, in the flesh, to lead and advise and correct and know exactly what to do? Well, however silly it sounds, that's what the Master said, and that is therefore the fact. But how, when we are at the very bottom of the valley, do we constructively grasp the truth of this amazing claim that the Holy Spirit is as much of a living presence with us as Jesus was with the disciples?

I'm no expert in these matters, but I do have a suggestion for my brothers and sisters in would-be discipleship. I know how we sometimes crouch fearfully behind locked doors, convinced that if we open up again we'll get something wrong again, and therefore there's no point. But let's not assume that we'll only find God in the unsafe outside. May I gently suggest that it is in the centre of that very locked place inside us that the Spirit of Jesus might suddenly come, as he came to Thomas and the other disciples two thousand years ago, and say, 'Peace be with you.'

Jesus is very kind. Let's pause and listen for him.

Pray with me

Father, we come to sit at your feet now, a straggling, motley crew of men, women and children who can't help seeing ourselves as very poor disciples, not just in the eyes of the world, but in your eyes as well…

Why are you smiling, Father?

We can't do it, you see. We can't be the shining band of light-filled spirits that we wanted to be for you. Little things some of us have managed, small achievements—half achievements, a bit of an attempt, or nothing at all…

Why are you smiling at us like that, Father?

We wondered if there was something we could do as a group, rather than on our own. We're a bit nervous on our own. If we put everything we've got together, there might be something there worth having, mightn't there? We couldn't do worse than we've done so far…

Why are you holding out your arms to us, Father?

We're truly sorry to have been so useless. We've all agreed that we're not really Christian material at all…

Why are you smiling and weeping at the same time, Father?

Questioning

Lost in the crowd?

Now Jesus' mother and brothers came to see him, but they were not able to get near him because of the crowd. Someone told him, 'Your mother and brothers are standing outside, wanting to see you.' He replied, 'My mother and brothers are those who hear God's word and put it into practice.'
LUKE 8:19–21

Near the cross of Jesus stood his mother, his mother's sister, Mary the wife of Clopas, and Mary Magdalene. When Jesus saw his mother there, and the disciple whom he loved standing near by, he said to his mother, 'Dear woman, here is your son,' and to the disciple, 'Here is your mother.' From that time on, this disciple took her into his home.
JOHN 19:25–27

G.K. Chesterton said that a paradox could be defined as 'the truth standing on its head'. This seems to me to be particularly applicable to Jesus, who came to turn the world upside down. I have always found his—apparent—contradictions extremely interesting and instructive. The truth retains its substance but changes its shape, because the doors (us) through which it must pass are so variable in height and width and general accessibility. Here is an example of that principle, and it might be a helpful one for those of us who fear that our individuality is swallowed up in the great salvation plan.

The story from Luke used to upset me very much when I was little. Fancy rotten old Jesus telling everyone he hadn't got a mum after all she'd been through with him! I got quite indignant on her behalf. Wanting to make some great religious point was no excuse for virtually disowning your own mother, was it? And what about his brothers? They must have been *really* upset.

Imagine it, I thought. You turn up outside the place where he's talking away nineteen to the dozen as usual, you send in a nice friendly message to say that his mother and brothers are waiting to see him, and some po-faced minion comes out with a message to say that he hasn't got a mother or brothers, because everyone who does what God wants can be his mother and brothers. To my childish mind it seemed likely that, on hearing this, Mary would have marched in, arms akimbo, and given him a piece of her mind.

'I'll give you *everyone*!' That's what I reckoned she would probably have said.

Time adjusted this grossly irreverent view, of course. As I grew up and read the Bible with more awareness, I sensed that Mary, quiet and wise, would simply have stored away this saying of her son's with all the other strange jigsaw pieces that she had collected over the years. Something about the Gospel accounts suggested to me that Jesus and his mother had enjoyed a deep, warm, eye-catching-across-the-room sort of relationship.

Then I encountered the above passage from John's Gospel, and as I read about this tender, last-minute provision for his mother's future I realized something else about Jesus. Maybe everyone could be his mother, but this was the first one he'd ever had, and he loved her. He was truly man, and he loved her.

> *'I have no mother.'*
> *'Mother, behold your son.'*

I had glimpsed for the first time the amazing truth that the Jesus who produced cosmic truths, dire warnings and spiritual bombshells, and the Jesus who remembered his mother's welfare at the time of his greatest agony, were one and the same person. For the first time in my life I felt that my individuality—my sense of self—was safe in the hands of God. We are not just units in the salvation package, but warm, complex, needy human beings, who are known, loved and cared for by him in special, separate ways.

Sometimes it doesn't feel like that though, does it?

Pray with me

Lord Jesus, when you spoke to your mother from the cross, you didn't say, 'My grace is sufficient for you—good luck, see you in heaven.' You gave her a flesh-and-blood person to look after her and be a son to her in your place. Lord, some of us are feeling very lost and insignificant in the Church. We need to know that as well as saving the universe, you care for us individually. We don't mind how that happens, but if there's a person who could offer us a relationship that you would bless and approve, don't let our fears and inhibitions get in the way, please. I see you on the cross now in my mind's eye. You are in great pain, but when you catch sight of me your expression lightens for a moment. You will never leave me or forsake me, but there is something practical I need to do in the meantime. Your voice is weak with pain so I must listen very hard to hear what you're saying...

Children of the night

Now there was a man of the Pharisees named Nicodemus, a member of the Jewish ruling council. He came to Jesus at night and said, 'Rabbi, we know you are a teacher who has come from God. For no one could perform the miraculous signs you are doing if God were not with him.' In reply Jesus declared, 'I tell you the truth, no one can see the kingdom of God unless he is born again.' 'How can a man be born when he is old?' Nicodemus asked. 'Surely he cannot enter a second time into his mother's womb to be born!' Jesus answered, 'I tell you the truth, no one can enter the kingdom of God unless he is born of water and the Spirit.'

JOHN 3:1–5

I suspect that, throughout history, a surprisingly large section of the Christian Church has only visited Jesus by night. In the heartsick early hours, or at times when the world has receded like a tide, they tiptoe warily into his presence, bringing with them the same burning acknowledgment of who he is, and the same searching questions, as Nicodemus brought two thousand years ago.

This army of secret admirers has probably included every class, race and type of person that ever existed, but I would like, just for a moment, to think about the young people of this age, and the difficulties they face in publicly relating to Jesus.

We adults don't help. I know that there have been times when I would have cheerfully exchanged all ideals of reality and integrity for the comfortable knowledge that my children were uncomplicated, incurious, card-carrying members of a chorus-singing, sausage-sizzling, sex-avoiding, Bible-studying, evangelical church youth group. There's nothing wrong with all those things, of course. Some of them are very right. But my concern was not actually for their relationship with Jesus.

I just wanted them out of harm's way so that I could find peace of mind.

You can't always have your parental cake and eat it. Many parents bring their children up to believe that it's all right to question and test, and be who they are. They may not have had some kind of grand organized plan, and they may have made horrendous mistakes from time to time, but they do want their offspring to have those qualities and that freedom. Their children might not, therefore, be the kind of kids who will ever be safely slotted into the sort of formal situation that I described (caricatured) just now. Many unchurched children will certainly have encountered God in the course of their lives, and their parents may be asking his blessing on them constantly, but perhaps, for the time being at least, they will be visiting Jesus by night, and he has to be trusted to deal with them. I think many of us would be astonished to learn how much is happening in the hearts and minds of the non-attending young people who cause us so much concern.

I would hate anyone to think that I was expressing anti-Church views. I belong to one myself, and I support everything that it does. Some youth groups are truly excellent and relevant. But my heart aches for the vast numbers of young people from both Christian and non-Christian families who simply cannot fit into such a situation *and* go on being who they are.

Christianity is *not* defined by the morning or the evening services, however good and necessary they might be.

Christianity is *not* defined by a way of speaking or dressing or doing religious things or aiming for vaguely middle-class norms.

Christianity is *not* defined by membership of the school Christian Union, however genuine, hard-working and prayerful.

Christianity is *not* defined by witnessing to classmates, however admirable and right that may sometimes be.

Christianity is *not* about teenagers making their parents feel safe by conforming to a particular subculture.

Christianity is about an encounter with God. It's about the need to turn from the negative past. It's about the need to be embraced by the warm and excited forgiveness of the Father. It's about discovering that it is possible to start again—to be born again. It's about understanding just a little of the sacrifice that Jesus made in dying on the cross. It's about establishing a lasting friendship with that same risen Jesus.

We can teach a young person some of these things, but the real negotiations have to be carried out privately between himself or herself and the Master, and sometimes that has to happen secretly, in the night.

Meanwhile, those of us who are worried will go on praying, and do our best to trust him.

Pray with me

We cry out to you for our young people, Father—not that they should conform to cultural or institutional expectations, but that they should meet you, Lord. That's what we want. Whether they come by conventional or eccentric routes is of no consequence. What matters is that they come to you with the needs and questions and problems that only you can deal with. Some of our churches are truly representing you, but many have become museums of tedium. We adults have allowed that to happen and we ask your forgiveness. We want to change things for the better. In the meantime, protect and watch over those who have drifted away, Father. When they come to you by night, may they learn how much you love them. Amen.

Through gritted teeth

'But I tell you who hear me: Love your enemies, do good to those who hate you, bless those who curse you, pray for those who ill-treat you. If someone strikes you on one cheek, turn to him the other also. If someone takes your cloak, do not stop him from taking your tunic. Give to everyone who asks you, and if anyone takes what belongs to you, do not demand it back. Do to others as you would have them do to you. If you love those who love you, what credit is that to you? Even "sinners" love those who love them. And if you do good to those who are good to you, what credit is that to you? Even "sinners" do that. And if you lend to those from whom you expect repayment, what credit is that to you? Even "sinners" lend to "sinners", expecting to be repaid in full. But love your enemies, do good to them, and lend to them without expecting to get anything back. Then your reward will be great, and you will be sons of the Most High, because he is kind to the ungrateful and wicked. Be merciful, just as your Father is merciful.'

Luke 6:27–36

These famous words of Jesus come ringing down through the years like a great bell proclaiming triumph and warning at the same time.

It proclaims triumph because the principle of forgiveness towards enemies still works and operates among those who are serious about wanting to follow and obey Jesus. Sometimes it has to be done through gritted teeth and with grindingly honest reservations, but wherever genuine attempts to be loving are brought face to face with hostility and hatred, a miracle of reconciliation is made possible.

The warning is for those who persist in a policy of aggression and revenge despite claiming to be adherents to the Christian faith. This is true on all levels, of course. My refusal to snap out of the carefully nurtured sulk with which I am childishly responding to my wife's latest major crime is no different in essence from more major conflicts, and we shall all answer to the same judge.

How tragic it is, though, that at so many points in history, and in so many parts of the world, the Bible has actually been used to justify murder and torture and war and repression. I have, for example, visited and spoken in both South Africa and Northern Ireland. The body of Christ in those countries makes an enormous difference for good, but, in both cases, I could only guess at the grief and anger of God over the way in which so-called Christianity has gone hand in hand with violence. Those who wanted war at all costs have gone into battle with a Bible in one hand and a gun in the other, and they understand neither.

Bibles and rifles
Handled by amateurs
Paper and metal
Tear us apart.
Fixing their sights
On the heart of reality
Bibles and rifles
There from the start.
Rifles and Bibles
Crashing through history
Leather and wood
Wounding and tears
Aiming and blaming
Shattering mystery
Rifles and Bibles
Ring in our ears.
Bibles and rifles
Rifles and Bibles
Bibles and trifles
Foibles and rifles

Rifles and Bibles
Bibles and rifles
Handled by amateurs
Ring in our ears.

None of us can afford to judge anyone else, and we do well to fear the wrath of God if we refuse to forgive. Why? Because, as Jesus so clearly tells us, here and elsewhere in the Bible, if we do not forgive our enemies, God will *not* forgive us.

Pray with me

Loving heavenly Father, I want to try to tackle this business of loving enemies. First of all I'm going to sit quietly here for a few minutes and go through a mental list of the folk whom I would call my enemies. Help me to be really honest. It's so easy to leave out people whom I've pushed from my consciousness because the very thought of them is too much for me to handle: people who I wish were dead; people who hurt me when I was little; people who have humiliated me in front of others; people who rejected me. I don't want to leave anyone out. I'll go through that list now. Let's do that...

I've done it, Lord. There are rather a lot, and some of them I really hate. But you made it quite clear that you can't forgive me if I don't forgive them, so I'll start the process, even if it takes a long time to mean it. Love them for me, Lord, and please accept my prayers for their welfare and safety. Soften my hard heart as the days go by, until I begin to see them through your eyes. Thank you for forgiving me. Amen.

The unacceptable alternative

'Once again, the kingdom of heaven is like a net that was let down into the lake and caught all kinds of fish. When it was full, the fishermen pulled it up on the shore. Then they sat down and collected the good fish in baskets, but threw the bad away. This is how it will be at the end of the age. The angels will come and separate the wicked from the righteous and throw them into the fiery furnace, where there will be weeping and gnashing of teeth. 'Have you understood all these things?' Jesus asked.
MATTHEW 13:47–51

Do you believe there is a place called hell? Does the idea of hell frighten you? Does it frighten you more or less than oblivion?

Whatever your answers to those questions might be, it is very hard to ignore the passionate urgency with which Jesus set about saving us from it. In fact, if hell is an illusion, it's difficult to see the point of Jesus coming at all. Why preach the gospel? Why warn people? Why talk about salvation? The debate about whether an all-loving, all-powerful God could possibly consign anybody to everlasting separation is all very well, but the fact is that Jesus came to show us how to avoid such a dismal end. Shall we ignore him?

Of course we musn't ignore him, but neither must we ignore the fact that the parable of the prodigal son comes from the same source, nor the fact that far more people are drawn to God by the power of love than were ever driven to him by the fear of hell. God loved the world with such a passion that he became astonishingly vulnerable so that we could be saved—a baby at the mercy of the world.

How can we understand hell? I don't think I understand it at all, but when I reach into the darkness of this incomprehension I find that my fingers touch something.

When I was small and confused (long before I became big and confused), I used to create my own little hell at times. For some perverse reason I found it more satisfying to be miserable than happy at certain times. Let me give you an example.

One winter night, after my two brothers and I had gone to bed, my mother called up the stairs to say that something very interesting was on the television (probably a nature programme) and that we could all get up and come down to watch it. My two brothers wrapped themselves in blankets and stumbled happily down the stairs to enjoy this unexpected treat. There *was* something very special about being 'up' after bedtime, especially in the winter when big chunks of (delivered!) coal burned in the open fireplace until they were hot enough to be split into flaming fragments with the old brass-handled poker that belonged in my grandmother's house before she died. It was cosy in the dining-room at those times.

So why did I refuse to go down to this place that was bright and friendly and nice? Why did I stay in my bed in the dark, weeping copiously because I wasn't in the place where I wanted to be? I could have been there. I had been invited to go there. I had only to leave my bed and take a few steps and I would *be* there. I can still recall the puzzlement in my mother's voice as she asked me why I was crying—and why, she queried with bewilderment, if it was because I wasn't downstairs, didn't I *come* downstairs? I couldn't answer her then and I have no neat answers now. Maybe I'll have to sort all that out one day.

But, for now, I offer you this story simply as a small image of hell.

Another, even more loving parent, calls and calls and calls in the night for his children to be with him in a good place, but countless numbers of them do not choose to come, and, to his great sorrow, confine themselves to limitless darkness, where they can be heard weeping and gnashing their teeth.

Pray with me

Lord Jesus, some people are trying to tell us that there can't be a hell because God loves us too much ever to put anyone there. I have travelled that road myself in the past. Oh, Lord, I am so sorry that we have discounted your life and death in this way. The truth is that your Father loved us so much that he created a means by which everyone can be saved from hell. Your passion is not wasted, Jesus. If you had to die to rescue me from whatever hell is, then I don't want to go there, and it frightens me.

We hear you calling, Father. Heal those who can't respond, and show us how we can communicate the urgency of your invitation without leaving out either the love or the danger. Amen.

Role-play

You are all sons of God through faith in Christ Jesus, for all of you who
were baptized into Christ have clothed yourselves with Christ. There is
neither Jew nor Greek, slave nor free, male nor female, for you are all one
in Christ Jesus. If you belong to Christ, then you are Abraham's seed, and
heirs according to the promise.

GALATIANS 3:26–29

I'm so glad that Paul included the bit about there being neither 'male
nor female' in Christ Jesus—not because I don't appreciate the
difference—believe me, I do—but because I fear that I fail to fulfil
some traditional expectations of THE MALE. No, I'm sorry. No lurid
revelations. I'm talking about home maintenance. I can change a plug
and waft a paintbrush about, but that's it. When it comes to most
other practical tasks I have to live in the mystery. And it gets no better,
because when I do decide to tackle a new job, I usually have to visit a
local DIY shop for tools or materials, and that does bad things to my
confidence. This is what happens.

As I enter timidly, the proprietor of the shop, a square, rather cross-
looking man with the sleeves of his checked shirt rolled up, is always
—*always*—carrying a wooden barrel full of long canes from one side
of the shop to the other. Don't ask me why—he just always is. As I
advance nervously, he puts his burden down and clicks his tongue in
irritation. He is annoyed because he was well into the rhythm of
carrying his barrel to and fro across the shop and now I've spoiled it.
He faces me and mimes a man holding a wheelbarrow.

'Yes?'

I name the tool I need, trying to look like the sort of person who
has competently worn one out and now needs another. Thank goodness I know exactly what I want. He sniffs.

'Plain or calibrated?'

What's that? Plain or what? I don't know! Oh, help, I don't know! Sound as if you *do* know.

'Err, better be plain, I think.'

'Plain—right.'

He shifts seventeen heavy boxes away from the base of a wall-unit, then fetches a stepladder from outside. The tool I need seems to be at the very back of the very highest shelf. All the things I buy are kept there. He climbs the ladder. Balancing on one foot, he jams his head between the ceiling and the top of the unit, contorting his face and grunting painfully as he locates the tool at the farthest extension of his reach. He ends up sweaty and dusty, and swears when he knocks a paper packet of tacks all over the floor on his way down. Sighing and puffing, he takes the stepladder back, replaces the seventeen heavy boxes, clears up the tacks, then turns to me. I am about to take my purchase when he speaks.

'Upstairs job then, is it?'

It's not! Oh, heavens, it's not! Shall I just take the plain one and pretend it's what I want? No. Be brave. Don't jabber.

'No, err, actually, it's a downstairs job. Err, sorry…'

He stares incredulously, then turns to catch the eye of a small, fat, balding, red-faced man in blue overalls who is holding the tiniest glowing remnant of a hand-rolled cigarette between his thumb and forefinger. This man has been sitting on the same stool by the counter, smoking the same cigarette, since the shop opened a generation ago. They shake their heads at each other in pleasurable disbelief, staggered by my idiocy. The proprietor speaks again.

'Calibrated you want, then.'

I cringe and twist with embarrassment. The red-faced man watches fatly. Smoke curls up from his hand.

'Err, yes. Yes, that's right—calibrated.'

After one brief, yearning glance at his barrel of canes, the proprietor sighs, and gets started on the seventeen heavy boxes…

Pray with me

Lord, some of us suffer genuine distress because we can't fit easily into the roles that are traditional in our society. I know there have been times in my own life when other people's ideas of maleness have made me feel isolated and miserable. When I was younger I disliked or denied whole areas of myself, because they didn't seem to fit in with the stereotypes that were presented to me. Nowadays, I don't have that kind of problem very much, but I know an awful lot of people do. I want to pray for them today, Father. I want to ask you to lead them gently into learning that whatever they are is valuable, and that, in the last analysis, the only thing that really matters is what you think of them—and you don't make these simplistic distinctions. Oh, and lead them to good friends, Father. Amen.

Fear of landing

John's disciples came and took his body and buried it. Then they went and told Jesus. When Jesus heard what had happened, he withdrew by boat privately to a solitary place. Hearing of this, the crowds followed him on foot from the towns. When Jesus landed and saw a large crowd, he had compassion on them and healed their sick. As evening approached, the disciples came to him and said, 'This is a remote place, and it's already getting late. Send the crowds away, so that they can go to the villages and buy themselves some food.' Jesus replied, 'They do not need to go away. You give them something to eat.' 'We have here only five loaves of bread and two fish,' they answered. 'Bring them here to me,' he said. And he directed the people to sit down on the grass. Taking the five loaves and the two fish and looking up to heaven, he gave thanks and broke the loaves. Then he gave them to the disciples, and the disciples gave them to the people. They all ate and were satisfied, and the disciples picked up twelve basketfuls of broken pieces that were left over. The number of those who ate was about five thousand men, besides women and children.

MATTHEW 14:12–21

Some fears are fully justified, and the fear of total commitment to God is a good example. A decision to work for the kingdom should be a very tough decision to make, because the demands can be impossibly high by human standards. Some modern evangelists seem to have forgotten the emphasis that Jesus placed on 'cost'. The Son of God certainly didn't say, 'Just come, just come to Jesus,' in treacly, wheedling tones. In the fourteenth chapter of Luke's Gospel he uses strong metaphors of building and war in his teaching on the subject. Don't follow me, he was saying, unless you've sat down and hard-headedly counted what it will cost you. In this passage we see the kind of example he set.

It begins with Jesus receiving the news of his cousin's death and withdrawing in a boat to find a secluded place in which to grieve. But, sympathetic as the crowd might be, they are as greedy for his presence as music fans are for their idols in this age. They follow on foot and probably stand in a solid, silent phalanx on the shore of the lake, waiting for him to come. Jesus didn't have many breaks, and this one wasn't allowed to last very long.

I can be terribly lazy at times, but I do know how it feels to have two solid blocks of speaking engagements separated only by a plane journey.

> *I understand a fear of flying,*
> *Not much fun if things go wrong up there,*
> *Options narrow down to less than two.*
> *But I enjoy the peace of being nowhere,*
> *Fending off the food, sleeping through the film,*
> *Hating first-class passengers,*
> *Solving, yet again, the puzzle of the toilet doors.*
> *Best of all is being sure that those I left behind*
> *Are not about to suddenly appear,*
> *And those who wait will have to wait a while*
> *For words and nods and smiles of understanding.*
> *They are there and I am here,*
> *Suspended, dreaming, guiltless in the air.*
> *My fear is not of flying but of landing.*

The needy crowds claimed Jesus after his brief respite, and it was back to work again, healing, teaching and listening. By the time evening came you'd have thought he might be entitled to a bit of peace, but instead of accepting the disciples' suggestion that the crowd should be sent away to buy food in the local villages, he takes upon himself the responsibility for feeding them. Have you ever asked yourself how *long* it took to break off enough bread and fish to feed more than five thousand people? That was one time-consuming, hand-aching miracle!

Time for a rest? Not yet. The disciples were sent ahead in the boat while Jesus dismissed the crowd. How long did that take? If you've ever watched people descend on a speaker after a big rally, you'll *know* how long it takes. Finally, they'd all gone. Sleep now? No, it was time for essential prayer now. And if you read on, you'll see that the night was far from over. There was to be a little maritime rescue operation, and then—yes, you guessed it—the crowds again.

Not everyone is called to a life of grinding toil, because that is not what is always needed, and most of us couldn't handle it anyway. But the commitment to Christ that is asked of us if we want to be of any use *is* exactly the same, and we are right to fear it. The cost is very high.

Pray with me

Lord Jesus, sometimes we fantasize about doing great things for you, but, as with all fantasies, the reality is quite daunting. Most of us are incapable of making a total commitment immediately, but we want to want to give everything to you eventually. Take us step by step along this hard road of learning that serving you will cost all that we have and all that we are. Thank you for your unswerving devotion to your Father and to us when you were here in the flesh. Show us by your example how to work and rest and pray, so that we can be as useful as we are capable of being. Amen.

Victims of sarcasm

It was the third hour when they crucified him. The written notice of the charge against him read: THE KING OF THE JEWS. They crucified two robbers with him, one on his right and one on his left. Those who passed by hurled insults at him, shaking their heads and saying, 'So! You who are going to destroy the temple and build it in three days, come down from the cross and save yourself!' In the same way the chief priests and the teachers of the law mocked him among themselves. 'He saved others,' they said, 'but he can't save himself!'

MARK 15:25–31

Shall I tell you something that really infuriates me? When my wife and I are in the car (I don't drive, myself), we occasionally encounter a type of driver who will react to any small mistake that Bridget might make with a slow, heavy, pityingly censorious shake of the head.

'It's just too wearisomely awful,' the perpetrator of this ghastly sighing movement seems to be saying, 'that we mature, capable human beings have got to put up with lesser creatures like *you*, who certainly should *not* be allowed on the road, and have probably made as much mess of every other department of your life as you have of being in charge of a car.'

I've always wanted to drag one of these head-shakers out of his car, throw him on to the tarmac, kneel on his chest and force him to tell me at least three areas in which he is totally incompetent, so that I can shake *my* head censoriously at *him*.

You don't think I'm over-reacting, do you?

This may sound like trivia, but do you realize that the God who loved us enough to hang bleeding on that piece of wood we call the cross got exactly the same head-shaking treatment from those who passed by? He, who with one divine, totally competent snap of the fingers could have summoned twelve legions of angels to give the whole world the tarmac treatment, consented to die so that those who mocked his failure could live.

Pray with me

Dear Lord, today we bring to you a great throng of people who have a basic fear of relationships because they have been seriously injured and handicapped by the scorn and sarcasm of others. To my shame, I, because of my own feelings of insecurity and lack of worth, was certainly responsible for inflicting some of these injuries when I was younger. Place your hand on those injuries for me now, Father. I know you don't often change people suddenly into something they are not, but perhaps the healing will begin for them. Whisper softly to them the wonderful truth that Jesus knows how they feel, because he had to put up with it as well. Dear Jesus—thank you. Amen.

Hope

Lifted by love

After this, Jesus went out and saw a tax collector by the name of Levi sitting at his tax booth. 'Follow me,' Jesus said to him, and Levi got up, left everything and followed him. Then Levi held a great banquet for Jesus at his house, and a large crowd of tax collectors and others were eating with them. But the Pharisees and the teachers of the law who belonged to their sect complained to his disciples, 'Why do you eat and drink with tax collectors and "sinners"?' Jesus answered them, 'It is not the healthy who need a doctor, but the sick. I have not come to call the righteous, but sinners to repentance.'

LUKE 5:27–32

When I was sixteen I loathed myself. I hated my face and my body, I had been expelled from school for truancy, and I had neither a job nor any visible prospect of getting one. The chaos inside my head was quite frightening.

To make matters worse, I had developed a strategy of using scathing sarcasm in the conduct of my relationships with anyone who made me feel silly (that is, almost everyone).

Miserable and unpleasant, I was definitely the sort of lad my mother didn't want me to go around with.

Then I was introduced to a married couple who lived in a secluded cottage near Wadhurst. Their home was a place of log fires, oil lamps, interesting books, stimulating conversation and (as far as I was concerned) total acceptance. Murray and Vivienne took the loaves and fishes of my better self and believed in me so wholeheartedly that, in their presence at least, that better self flourished and grew to a point where I actually began to believe I could be worth something.

I find it very uncomfortable to remember how I viewed my relationship with Murray and Vivienne after I became a Christian. The three of us were accustomed to long, enjoyable conversations on every subject under the sun. We would talk happily into the early hours sometimes, sifting through various options for belief and commitment, without seriously considering the possibility that we might actually adopt any of them. They received the news of my conversion with little enthusiasm (for a number of reasons), and for a year or more we hardly met.

My discomfort is caused by the fact that it took over twenty years for me to realize that God gave me Murray and Vivienne at a time when I really did need to be 'saved' by their almost unconditional support. Conversion in the 1960s seemed to require a complete re-labelling of every experience that one had had in the past, or was having now. Thus, all preconversion relationships and events were 'non-Christian' and bad (unless they were specifically religious occasions which 'the Lord was using to bring one to faith'), whereas everything that occurred after conversion was 'Christian' and good. It seems extraordinary now that I could have assumed God's non-involvement in something as important as my relationship with the Staplehursts.

Murray and Vivienne were not Christians, nor was I when I first met them, but their unqualified support was the first and most practically effective step in the salvation of Adrian Plass. Nowadays I thank God properly for them and always will.

In Levi's case, the middle-men/women/persons were cut out altogether. His encouragement came from the Master in person. Jesus himself had said 'Follow me' to this man who would have been regarded by most folk as a rat. A great hope swelled in his heart. He was a failure in almost every way that really mattered, but the Lord believed in him.

What a banquet that must have been!

Pray with me

Father, there must be lots of Christians and non-Christians who, at this very moment, need the kind of support that I got from Murray and Vivienne. First of all, could we pray that as many as possible do find a place where they can learn to think a little more highly of themselves, and secondly, please nudge those of us who are in a position to offer hospitality into an awareness that you might need to use us. Let our focus be love rather than religion, Lord (I'm sure you chose Murray and Vivienne for me because they hadn't any kind of spiritual itch to scratch), and we'll keep our ears as open as possible to hear your voice leading and encouraging. Thank you so much for the people who do build others up, and please forgive me for sticking silly labels on your gifts. Amen.

Decay and renewal

I consider that our present sufferings are not worth comparing with the glory that will be revealed in us. The creation waits in eager expectation for the sons of God to be revealed. For the creation was subjected to frustration, not by its own choice, but by the will of the one who subjected it, in hope that the creation itself will be liberated from its bondage to decay and brought into the glorious freedom of the children of God. We know that the whole creation has been groaning as in the pains of childbirth right up to the present time. Not only so, but we ourselves, who have the firstfruits of the Spirit, groan inwardly as we wait eagerly for our adoption as sons, the redemption of our bodies. For in this hope we were saved. But hope that is seen is no hope at all. Who hopes for what he already has? But if we hope for what we do not yet have, we wait for it patiently. In the same way, the Spirit helps us in our weakness. We do not know what we ought to pray, but the Spirit himself intercedes for us with groans that words cannot express. And he who searches our hearts knows the mind of the Spirit, because the Spirit intercedes for the saints in accordance with God's will.

ROMANS 8:18–27

I have always felt sickened by the inevitability of decay. This is mainly because of the way in which anything new that came into our house when I was a child was so rapidly swept into the maelstrom of damage and deterioration that seemed to characterize the way we lived. Everything died, became discoloured, stopped working, ran out, fell apart, became a disappointment, dwindled away to nothing. That's what my memory tells me, although I don't suppose it can have been as bad as that. I do know that the groaning tension of those days is still a part of me in both silly and important ways.

One absurdly trivial example is my inward refusal to believe that it's possible to buy a brand-new tin of shoe polish. We can't have used only *one* small tin of polish (the sort with the cherries on top) throughout my entire childhood, but that's how it seems when I look back. I knew the contours of that little container like the back of my hand. Every time I cleaned my shoes I scraped and pressed the brush against the grooves on the inside of the tin, looking for just one more tiny smear of polish to apply to my sensible, all-purpose, black school-shoes. It never ever occurred to me that new tins existed somewhere, full to the brim, and shining smooth on top when you turned the little lever at the side and pushed the lid off. Something in me is still, after all these years, quite agnostic about the proposition that polish is easily bought and replaced. You see, the child in me knows that it *cannot* be so, even when the adult tells him not to be so silly.

A predisposition to disappointment in relationships is a more serious legacy from that part of my life, but it operates in exactly the same way. Because of continual evidence that happy situations not only do not last, but usually descend into conflict or sulking, I find it extremely hard to enjoy the good times without expecting, or sometimes even provoking, a negative end to the day, or the trip, or the game, or the meal. That blinking little kid *knows* that everything's bound to go wrong.

Some shadows are very far-reaching and very damaging.

What hope? Well, God is very good at transfiguration (defined by the dictionary as 'making more beautiful'). My dreary conviction that everything is sure to end up horrible is not at all beautiful, but perhaps God is inviting me to redirect these intimations of destruction into an understanding of this passage from Romans.

I think I unconsciously anticipated this invitation the other day when I was walking on the Downs with a friend. I commented on the difference between being up there in the morning, when the world seems breathtakingly vigorous and confident, whatever the weather, and walking the same paths at dusk when the sun has gone and a chill of shame and sadness creeps over those gently rolling hills. They, with the rest of creation, have been in bondage to decay for so long. At such times it is easy to believe that the groaning of the natural world is audible.

The earth is waiting for Eden to return—for the time when there is no death and no decay. We are waiting for the same thing. We want to walk with God in the cool of the afternoon just as we were meant to.

Until then we groan to God with groans that words cannot express. My childhood can never return in the form that I would have liked, but maybe God will help me to set that aside, and concentrate on the childhood of the world, which *will* be renewed.

When I was small
I didn't know the world had fallen long ago
I stumbled often, fell from trees
Enjoyed the pride of bloodied knees
And banks were made for rolling down
Or sliding when the snow had come
My bones would bend more easily
Even when they broke they mended soon
And people gave me things to cheer me up.
I once went sledging with a friend at night
He didn't trust the moon and he was right
It slipped away as we began our ride
But I was glad, I loved the dark
For all I cared we could have sledged into eternity
I wished that pale hissing dream would never end
It did—I have the scars
I still have all the scars from all the falls
And mainly on my knees
But somewhere deep inside
Where no one ever sees
I have some other scars that never seem to heal
The cause of them I cannot now recall, but then,
I didn't know the world had fallen long ago
When I was small.

Pray with me

Father, may the deep shadows of the past be dispelled by the light of your new creation. Amen.

Cuddling the kids

People were bringing little children to Jesus to have him touch them, but the disciples rebuked them. When Jesus saw this, he was indignant. He said to them, 'Let the little children come to me, and do not hinder them, for the kingdom of God belongs to such as these. I tell you the truth, anyone who will not receive the kingdom of God like a little child will never enter it.' And he took the children in his arms, put his hands on them and blessed them.

MARK 10:13–16

People who have entered into the grave error of hearing me speak publicly more than once cannot fail to have noticed that the subjects of children and childhood lie very close to my heart. I have four children myself, who, over the years, have brought me great brimming buckets full of joy, pain and revelation. Before becoming a writer I worked with children in the care of the local authority, and recently I have felt more able to face and address the child that I used to be, and who still lives in me. Just occasionally I've even managed to coax that worried, skinny little kid with his pudding-basin haircut out for an excursion into the world where I try to live as an adult. He's just beginning to trust me...

In this passage from Mark's Gospel we find the disciples doing what they always did most consistently—getting it wrong. Life must have been quite bewildering for these twelve spiritually press-ganged itinerants. Every time they thought they'd worked out where Jesus was coming from, it turned out that they hadn't.

My own personal favourite among such incidents is the one where Jesus is not welcomed in a particular locality, and the disciples, filled with the sort of cosmic indignation that must have seemed fitting to their elevated position in the universe, said, 'Shall we call down fire from heaven on this village, Lord?' Is it wicked of me to imagine the Monty Pythonesque weariness with which Jesus pushed the hair back off his forehead and replied, 'No, we will *not* call down fire from heaven on this village…'?

Here, they are getting it wrong in connection with children. Like some fussy committee, the disciples are intent on shooing away the untidy, unimportant element in the crowd so that the Master doesn't waste his time on trivial pursuits. How could they have known that in the eyes of those children Jesus saw some shining memory or reflection of heaven and home? He was indignant. He wanted to cuddle the children and bless them—so he did. I have no doubt at all that the disciples simply reversed the direction of their officiousness at this point, and sternly proceeded to herd every child in sight towards their Master. Most of us learn very slowly, don't we?

I would like to tell you that ever since I was converted at the age of sixteen, the aspiring disciple in me has been preventing that skinny kid I mentioned earlier from coming to be cuddled and blessed by Jesus. I think I have been afraid that his formlessness, his pain and his unimportance were poor qualifications for intimate contact with the Master. I am sure I have been wrong. Of course, I would like to be a maturing, organized, competent disciple of Christ, but I have a new awareness that every now and then the child needs to slip past the adult to be taken into the arms of Jesus and simply held for a while.

The way forward is the way back, and the way back will take us to the place where we have always wanted to be. For when we look into the eyes of the child that God loves in us, we will see the same reflection of heaven that Jesus saw two thousand years ago in the eyes of those Jewish children who got their ears clipped by the grown-ups for trying to get near to God.

Pray with the children

Dear Jesus, I'm speaking on behalf of some of the children who hide inside your grown-ups every Sunday in church. We've been good for a very long time now, even though we don't really like sitting in rows doing boring things and not being noticed much. When we get excited we have to hide even further down. When we get sad we're not allowed to cry out loud because it will disturb other people and they will think bad things about the grown-ups we live in. Jesus, can you find a way to make them let us out, please? Some of us haven't been cuddled for a very long time now, and we think that's what children need. Speak to them for us, Lord. Bless you. Amen.

Giving and getting

As Jesus started on his way, a man ran up to him and fell on his knees before him. 'Good teacher,' he asked, 'what must I do to inherit eternal life?' 'Why do you call me good?' Jesus answered. 'No one is good—except God alone. You know the commandments: "Do not murder, do not commit adultery, do not steal, do not give false testimony, do not defraud, honour your father and mother."' 'Teacher,' he declared, 'all these I have kept since I was a boy.' Jesus looked at him and loved him. 'One thing you lack,' he said. 'Go, sell everything you have and give to the poor, and you will have treasure in heaven. Then come, follow me.' At this the man's face fell. He went away sad, because he had great wealth.

MARK 10:17–22

Over the years, I have passed through many phases of response to this famous story. One of the earliest was simple irritation with Jesus for refusing to stretch a point and let the young man hang on to his cash. Why did he let the poor chap walk away sorrowing when a slight curving of the rules could have had him dancing with delight? That's definitely what I would have done, wouldn't you? After all, and I'm sure Judas would have gone along with this, the money could have come in very handy to support the ongoing team ministry. Not having anywhere to lay your head was all right as a public statement of principle, but it would have been nice to have a little nest-egg put aside for when things got *really* tough. Fancy missing out on the recruitment of a good man for almost no reason at all. This stubbornness on the part of Jesus really annoyed me. Heaven must have trembled, don't you think?

'Look out, God!' the angels will have shouted. 'Adrian Plass is annoyed because Jesus wouldn't let the rich young man keep his money!'

'Oh, no!' cries God, ducking behind his own throne. 'Tell him I'm out if he comes round.'

As the years pass, I am forced to the conclusion that I may have been a mite hasty in reacting so negatively (great relief in heaven as God comes out from behind his throne). There are two things about the incident that I know now, but didn't know then.

First, it is a good example (and the Gospels abound in them) of the honesty and directness which characterized Jesus' dealings with men and women. How we need that kind of fearlessly loving assertiveness in the Church today.

Secondly, I know now that a deep and doomladen fear was the underlying reason for my cross response to Jesus' handling of that particular situation. I was afraid—and the same fear is by no means foreign to me now—that Jesus would ask me to sell all that I had and give it to the poor. I'm not necessarily talking about money, you understand. I wasn't a rich young man when I first read the story, and I'm not a rich middle-aged man now. Our riches come in many wild and wonderful forms, and they are always in the same place as our hearts. My fear was, and is, that God constantly asks me to give away, or at the very least to loosen my grip on, the thing that I value most— the thing that makes me feel safe and OK. As long as that thing is not Jesus, it will be demanded of me, and I would be a fool not to give it.

But I *am* afraid.

I heard a story in Australia that helped me.

A young mentally handicapped girl called Minnie was sitting in church with a member of staff from the place where she lived. The time had come for the collection plate to be passed around. Minnie had her own purse, with her own money in it, but she wasn't sure how much she should give. Leaning over, she whispered to her helper, 'How much do you think I ought to put in?'

'That's between you and God, Minnie,' replied the lady. 'You must decide.'

Minnie opened her purse. There were only two coins in there. One was a fifty-cent piece, a large coin, worth about 22 pence in UK money. The other was a two-dollar piece, tiny in comparison but worth four times as much. Minnie took out this smaller coin, and held it in her fist as she prayed with her eyes screwed tight shut. Her prayer must have been answered. She opened her eyes, plunged the two-dollar piece back into her purse, drew out the fifty-cent coin and held it up to show her helper.

'No!' she said, her eyes shining. 'The *big* one for Jesus!'

What this gentle little parable suggests is that if we give away the thing that seems most valuable to us, we may, by God's grace, be left with something that always was immeasurably more valuable than we could have realized or imagined.

Pray with me

Lord, I need some help here. First of all, I'm not at all confident about being able to identify the thing that I value most. Here's a list of front-running candidates:

The love and companionship of my wife, family and friends.

The pursuit of top-level priorities involving security and love in my immediate family.

The choice of where I shall live and the kind of work I shall do. I want to go on being a writer.

Opportunities to have large expansive meals accompanied by good wine, with people who make me relax.

Enough money to prevent the dreadful desolate feeling that comes when we haven't any at all.

The right to be offended and to demonstrate my upsetness by sulking or using some other negative ploy.

I know there's nothing wrong with any of these things in themselves, Lord (well, I suppose the last one's not too wonderful), but I don't want any of them to be at the top of the list. I want you to be there. I want to be as wise and as generous as Minnie. Help me, Father. Amen.

Heaven on earth?

'Do not let your hearts be troubled. Trust in God; trust also in me. In my Father's house are many rooms; if it were not so, I would have told you. I am going there to prepare a place for you. And if I go and prepare a place for you, I will come back and take you to be with me that you also may be where I am. You know the way to the place where I am going.' Thomas said to him, 'Lord, we don't know where you are going, so how can we know the way?' Jesus answered, 'I am the way and the truth and the life. No one comes to the Father except through me.'

John 14:1–6

When I'm in heaven
Tell me there'll be kites to fly,
The kind they say you can control
Although I never did for long,
The kind that spin and spin and spin and spin
Then sulk and dive and die,
And rise again and spin again,
And dive and die and rise up yet again,
I love those kites.

When I'm in heaven
Tell me there'll be friends to meet,
In ancient oak-beamed Sussex pubs
Enfolded by the wanton Downs,
And summer evenings lapping lazily against the shore
Of sweet familiar little lands
Inhabited by silence or by nonsenses,
The things you cannot safely say in any other place,
I love those times.

When I'm in heaven
Tell me there'll be seasons when the colours fly,
Poppies splashing flame
Through dying yellow, living green,
And autumn's burning sadness that has always made me cry
For things that have to end.
For winter fires that blaze like captive suns
But look so cold when morning comes.
I love the way the seasons change.

When I'm in heaven
Tell me there'll be peace at last,
That in some meadow filled with sunshine
Filled with buttercups and filled with friends
You'll chew a straw and fill us in on how things really are,
And if there is some harm in laying earthly hope at heaven's door,
Or in the saying so,
Have mercy on my foolishness, dear Lord,
I love this world you made—it's all I know. Amen.

A job for life

When they had finished eating, Jesus said to Simon Peter, 'Simon son of John, do you truly love me more than these?' 'Yes, Lord,' he said, 'you know that I love you.' Jesus said, 'Feed my lambs.' Again Jesus said, 'Simon son of John, do you truly love me?' He answered, 'Yes, Lord, you know that I love you.' Jesus said, 'Take care of my sheep.' The third time he said to him, 'Simon son of John, do you love me?' Peter was hurt because Jesus asked him the third time, 'Do you love me?' He said, 'Lord, you know all things; you know that I love you.' Jesus said, 'Feed my sheep.'

JOHN 21:15–17

I felt intimidated by these verses. So many people who are much cleverer than me have written about them. When I feel defensive I become flippant. I found myself reflecting on the fact that the passage sounds like one of those pre-holiday conversations when you're trying to soft-soap a friend into looking after the family pets for a fortnight. I took the dog for a walk to clear my head, and now I'm back with a more serious thought.

In an earlier section we saw how wretched Peter felt after his three predicted denials, and I was trying to express some of the pain that we experience in the process of accepting that we are completely *known* by God. Here, though, is the other side of the coin.

In this famous post-breakfast dialogue, Jesus, in addition to knocking out those three denials like targets on a rifle range, is handing his friend a formidable pastoral responsibility. Later, Peter might well have reasoned as follows:

Jesus was always straight with me—too straight, I used to think. He called me Satan when I thought he'd be grateful.

When I said I'd never desert him, he told me I'd deny him three times, and he was right. He knows everything. Now he's given me a job to do, even though he knows me from the bottom of my sandals to the top of my head. That means he knows I can do it.

And, as we all know, he did it.

Pray with me

Lord, I get very confused and fearful about what I'm supposed to be doing and what I'm not supposed to be doing. Everyone seems to think something different about guidance, and I end up in a sort of mist. Help me to think back to the last time I felt confident that you had given me a task. Have I accomplished it? If I haven't, am I still working on it? Has it got buried under a mountain of false distractions? If you gave me the job, Lord, then I know, as Peter knew, that it can be done by me. Assist me in clearing away the rubbish, and if there is unfinished business between us that's hindering my work, tell me. Let's clear the decks and start again. Amen.

Dear Daddy...

For you did not receive a spirit that makes you a slave again to fear, but you received the Spirit of sonship. And by him we cry, *'Abba*, Father.'
ROMANS 8:15

When Bob Hope was asked if he thought he would qualify for heaven, he replied, 'Well, I sure hope I don't miss out on a technicality.'

A lot of the people that I meet have exactly that problem. What if their theology is deficient in some crucial area? Will the keeper of heaven's gate scan their personal statement of faith and, with a regretful shake of the head, announce that they've not quite made it, in the same way that a driving test is failed because of one trivial error? Theology maintains the purity of the divine stream, but love is the boat that carries us to Jesus. Have a good look at the picture on the following page.

Katy, aged six, sent this letter to me when I was touring South Africa on my own in 1993. It's a communication from a child to her father, and it contains some interesting features.

First of all, the 'theology' is appalling, isn't it? I wasn't in South America, was I? I was in South Africa. Next, the so-called representation of me is wildly inaccurate (anyone who thinks otherwise is in serious trouble). Everyone knows that I'm an old man with a beard.

Then there's the spelling. Since when was 'sposto' included in the Oxford Dictionary? Take a look at the lines of handwriting—they're all over the place, up and down like a roller-coaster. And what's happened to the address and the date and the telephone number? They're not there, are they? Kisses are all very well, but they don't *tell* you anything useful, do they? What kind of communication *is this*?

to Dad I hope you will rite to us wen you
get to south amerika I hope
you Like my pithcha it is sposto
LOOK LiRe You   I miss You
very mupch   Love from
             Katy

I'll tell you what kind of communication this is. It's the most wonderful letter any lonely father ever had from a beloved child. Do you seriously think that I would have wanted so much as a single letter to be changed, just for the sake of some boringly legalistic accuracy? No, of course not. Every kiss counted. Each tongue-protruding attempt to convey love touched my heart in that distant, troubled land.

Theology *is* important, but God needs to be loved like everyone else. Don't be afraid to climb on to his knee because you lack understanding. Daddies need kisses, and the rest can wait.

Pray with me

When we look at the erudition and learning of some Christians we can feel intimidated, Father. Do you really want to hear from us twits who can never quite remember where Ephesians is, and don't know if the Bible is supposed to be infallible or inerrant—or both—and aren't sure what the difference is anyway?

How silly we are to be put off by such things, Father. Teach us to love you from our hearts with innocence, enthusiasm and warmth. Help us to get back into the habit of just being with you and, above all, to understand that there is nothing sinful, inappropriate or proud about believing that you need the love of your children. Dear Father, teach us to love. Amen.

Playing to the gallery

The next day the great crowd that had come for the Feast heard that Jesus was on his way to Jerusalem. They took palm branches and went out to meet him, shouting, 'Hosanna!' 'Blessed is he who comes in the name of the Lord!' 'Blessed is the King of Israel!' Jesus found a young donkey and sat upon it, as it is written, 'Do not be afraid, O Daughter of Zion; see, your king is coming, seated on a donkey's colt.' At first his disciples did not understand all this. Only after Jesus was glorified did they realize that these things had been written about him and that they had done these things to him. Now the crowd that was with him had continued to spread the word that he had called Lazarus from the tomb, raising him from the dead. Many people, because they had heard that he had given this miraculous sign, went out to meet him. So the Pharisees said to one another, 'See, this is getting us nowhere. Look how the whole world has gone after him!'

JOHN 12:12–19

A friend, recently returned from a trip to Israel, showed me a photograph of the gate through which Jesus must have ridden when he entered Jerusalem. The arch is adorned with a large sign saying NO ENTRY. It is a sobering thought that if Jesus had come into the world in this age, his arrival in the city might have been seriously complicated by the ponderous presence of a uniformed traffic official, gazing dispassionately at his four-footed vehicle and saying, 'I'm sorry, sir, rules are rules, whoever you are. I'm afraid you'll have to go right round the city and come in through the one-way system just like everyone else.'

Here we see Jesus experiencing one of the few moments of public celebration that he was allowed during his earthly ministry. Those who feverishly advocate triumphal behaviour at all times might do worse than to study the variable pattern of the Master's emotional and spiritual life. Preceded by tears and followed by death, this rare triumph was brief enough, goodness knows, but all that mattered to him was its *rightness*. Jesus flatly refused all television and film offers. For three years he had rejected every opportunity to grasp the glory that men would have offered him, but this little capsule of joyful exuberance was part of the Father's plan and it must have warmed his heart. The right entry, at the right time, with the right *audience*.

Sometimes I wish I'd never started this book. I thought I knew—more or less—what my fears were. But there are layers below layers, aren't there? As soon as I began to think about 'audience', I realized that I have never properly faced my own dependence on a sort of phantom auditorium full of invisible people who exist only to applaud the soap opera of my life.

When I was younger it was far worse, of course. As a young teenager I didn't want to do or have anything for its own sake. I just wanted the 'badge'. I wanted to go out with a girl so that I could say I was going out with a girl. I wanted to go somewhere in an aeroplane so that I could chat nonchalantly about how it felt to fly. I wanted a smart watch, not to keep track of the time, which has never interested me very much, but so that people could see me looking at my impressive timepiece. I bought cigarettes so that I could exhale smoke through my nostrils while I gazed at the horizon in filmic close-ups as the final music swelled to a climax and a deeply moved audience gazed enthralled from their cinema seats. I was a twit. But I was probably a fairly average twit. Most people have gone through a similar stage, but most people grow up—don't they?

The thing that frightens me now is an awareness that these invisible onlookers are still having a profound effect on my life. Every now and then I do something significant or go somewhere interesting, and then discover a vacuum where normal satisfaction or enjoyment should be. I think I am waiting for applause. This habit—this addiction to audience—has damaged my capacity for immediate, vital encounters with life's events.

I want to be like Jesus. I want to be interested only in the approval of the Father. I want him to be my audience, but I will need healing before that reality can inhabit the whole country of my heart. There are still an awful lot of NO ENTRY signs that will have to be taken down.

Pray with me

Father, some of us are still dependent on the applause of the world, and because your approval is not enough of a reality, we can't quite kick the drug. We are taught so early in our lives, Lord, that the way other people see us is vitally important, and, of course, it is in a way, but Jesus said we would do better to store up treasure in heaven. He told us that you would reward us secretly if we do good to others secretly. This is not the way of the world, Father, but we understand that it's your way, so would you please heal us of our dependence on worldly applause, and open our ears to hear the angels cheering. Amen.

The hills of home

Now there were some Greeks among those who went to worship at the Feast. They came to Philip, who was from Bethsaida in Galilee, with a request. 'Sir,' they said, 'we would like to see Jesus.' Philip went to tell Andrew; Andrew and Philip in turn told Jesus. Jesus replied, 'The hour has come for the Son of Man to be glorified. I tell you the truth, unless a grain of wheat falls to the ground and dies, it remains only a single seed. But if it dies, it produces many seeds. The man who loves his life will lose it, while the man who hates his life in this world will keep it for eternal life. Whoever serves me must follow me; and where I am, my servant also will be. My Father will honour the one who serves me.'

JOHN 12:20–26

From early 1981 to late 1987 Bridget and I were involved in a late-night television epilogue programme called 'Company'. In the course of those seven years, sitting around an old kitchen table in the Maidstone studios of TVS, we met many people. Some were well known, while others were quite new to the comparatively small number of viewers who tuned in each night. To be quite honest, we preferred the prospect of meeting anonymous contributors because the private presentation of Christian 'celebrities' sometimes failed to match their public image (God forgive my arrogance—and my hypocrisy!).

David Watson, the much-loved evangelist and writer, was in no way a disappointment. The programmes we recorded with him were very enjoyable ones from our point of view, but we gained even more pleasure from the time spent preparing, eating and relaxing with David on the day before entering the studio. He was a man who seemed full of both joy and pain, together with an infectious enthusiasm for the God he had served so effectively.

It was a particularly poignant experience because David had already been diagnosed as suffering from the cancer that later caused his death. He seemed so well to us. By the time we met him, he had wrestled his way agonizingly from—as he put it—'wanting to stay but being willing to go', through to 'wanting to go but being willing to stay if he was healed'. The journey from the first of those statements to the second must have been rather like getting to the South Pole on foot, but in accomplishing it he was directly fulfilling the words of Jesus in this passage: 'Whoever serves me must follow me; and where I am, my servant also will be. My Father will honour the one who serves me.'

David was following in his Master's footsteps, and he will have been honoured for that. I feel quite sure that Jesus loved this world, and, as he faced the cancer of sin which was to enter his body on the cross, he must have had to make a similar journey of the will. If he didn't, he was not truly man.

Could I make that journey?

Could heaven become home while I'm still lodging on earth?

I fear not, but God is very ingenious, so I may be wrong. The following lines, which I wrote quite recently, are not true yet, but I pray that one day they will be.

Some other country
Claims me now,
But I will stay
Because we love this place,
And I can always see the hills of home
From top-floor windows,
But only if I climb the stairs.
I'd rather see the hills
Than say my prayers
At the bottom of the stairs.
Some other country
Lacking this beloved citizen
Whose straining eyes

Have never even seen the land where he belongs,
Except for distant hills
From top-floor windows,
When he climbs the stairs
With others who might share
Unwillingness to mumble prayers
At the bottom of the stairs.
Some other country
Where the builder waits
And faithfully prepares
The mansions we shall need,
All set among the hills
And all of them are made by hand
And all of them are home
And all of them are visited
And none of them need stairs.

Pray with me

Dear Lord, today I sense the warmth with which you look forward to the time when we can all be together in our real home. You know how it will be, but it's a bit cloudy for us. Every now and then, though, when we are in the middle of something beautiful, we feel a touch of homesickness for the place where we've never been. Thank you for preparing places for us. Thank you for the slow process of change in our thinking. We have feared that we might be refugees and aliens in the place where you are, but you are gradually filling us with an awareness of the citizenship of heaven that Jesus bought for us on the cross. Sometimes we long for the hills of home. Amen.

Under the spotlight

Then Jesus told them, 'You are going to have the light just a little while longer. Walk while you have the light, before darkness overtakes you. The man who walks in the dark does not know where he is going. Put your trust in the light while you have it, so that you may become sons of light.' When he had finished speaking, Jesus left and hid himself from them. Even after Jesus had done all these miraculous signs in their presence, they still would not believe in him. This was to fulfil the word of Isaiah the prophet: 'Lord, who has believed our message and to whom has the arm of the Lord been revealed?' For this reason they could not believe, because, as Isaiah says elsewhere, 'He has blinded their eyes and deadened their hearts, so they can neither see with their eyes, nor understand with their hearts, nor turn—and I would heal them.' Isaiah said this because he saw Jesus' glory and spoke about him. Yet at the same time many even among the leaders believed in him. But because of the Pharisees they would not confess their faith for fear they would be put out of the synagogue; for they loved praise from men more than praise from God.

JOHN 12:35–43

Let me tell you about three attempts to avoid the light.

The first involves a friend of mine whom I shall call Grace, an unmarried lady in her late 50s. Bridget and I were invited to eat with her one evening at the centuries-old house where she lives alone (apart from some very 'human' dogs). We accepted the invitation with enthusiasm. Grace's charming, somewhat lateral view of life promised an evening that would be interesting, at the very least. It was.

We turned up on the right evening (you don't know what an achievement that is for me) and were shown through two beautifully furnished rooms in the old house, accompanied by what seemed like a river of dogs, until we reached the kitchen door.

'We're eating in here,' said Grace, waving us through as she spoke.

The kitchen was a cave of darkness with three little spots of light arranged in a triangular pattern around the table that occupied the centre of the room. Bridget and I peered into the gloom surrounding this dimly lit island, but only the vaguest outlines of other objects were visible.

Grace, who must have been on a very heavy carrot diet, served our meal almost immediately, together with an excellent claret. The food was extremely good, but it took a bit of finding in the half-light. The candles that burned beside each place were not very big, and one vegetable looks very much like another in silhouette. Hunched over our plates, concentrating fiercely as we sought to identify the various elements in our meals, one side of each of our faces glowing orange in the flickering candlelight, we might have been posing for one of those Gothic paintings, to be entitled 'Ghouls Feasting'. I tried to catch Bridget's eye, but I couldn't see it. I cleared my throat.

'Err, it's a bit dark, isn't it, Grace? Nice atmosphere and all that, but a bit err… dark.'

From the other end of the cave, Grace replied calmly.

'Yes, I know, it's deliberate. I didn't want you to see what a disgusting state the kitchen's in.'

'But you don't mind us knowing that it's in a disgusting state?' queried Bridget, in mystified tones.

'Oh, no,' said Grace, 'just so long as you can't see it. That's all that matters.'

What do you call that? Honest deception, perhaps?

The second piece of light evasion was by another friend, Tim by name, a Christian believer, who started a new and very satisfying job, only to discover that his colleagues, who were all very pleasant, had quite aggressively negative attitudes towards Christians and Christianity. In their view, you could be just about anything, from a scientologist to a frog-worshipper, as long as you didn't get caught up with all that cringe-making stuff about Jesus.

Tim hadn't been able to bring himself to tell his workmates the awful truth, and every day that went by made it more difficult. He found a little relief by telling himself that it was actually better for them to get to know him first, so that 'his works could reveal his faith', but I didn't think Tim seemed too comfortable with this rationalization. I wonder why not? He still hasn't told them, by the way.

My third character in this gallery of nocturnal personalities is me. I feel so ashamed when I remember this incident.

I was at stage school in Bristol at the time, oscillating wildly between the excesses produced by, on the one hand, fairly fanatical evangelicalism and, on the other, the whole business of being away from home for the first time in the artificially amoral ethos of theatre school. One evening, clutching my big black Bible and drinking coffee in the university union building up the road from the school, I got into conversation with a student who had made the foolish mistake of asking me what 'book' I was reading. Being in spiritual mode on that particular occasion, I let him have it right between the eyes. He was impressed. I could tell he was impressed. When I left (the fact that I left before he did must have been significant), he was pondering deeply. I rejoiced appropriately.

I saw him again less than a week later. This time he walked into a pub where I was firmly entrenched in my *non*-spiritual mode, together with a few associates who had never pretended to have a spiritual mode in the first place. We were all more than a little the worse for wear. I greeted the newcomer boisterously. I knew I'd met him somewhere before, but for the moment I couldn't remember where. His eyes brightened when he first spotted me, but faded gradually as he took in my semi-drunken state and the general quality of the conversation. Then I remembered who he was, and I felt ashamed. I don't think I ever saw him again.

Following Jesus is very costly. Part of the cost is being seen for what we are under the floodlight of his perfectness. Many of us fear, quite justifiably, that our flaws and foolishnesses will be exposed if we stand too close to him. Well, of course they will, and they should be. It's him we're advertising—not us. When I spoke to that chap in the union building I shouldn't have crinkled my eyes and hinted at hidden mystical depths. I should have made it clear that I was a failing follower, and not given the impression that I was teetering on the brink of sainthood. Nowadays I would try to be me.

Will Tim ever come clean?

Do we dare to turn the lights on in the kitchen, and still claim to be followers of Jesus? I'm not quite sure how I would answer that question.

Pray with me

Father, occasionally I think it would be easier to give up my faith than to stand in the light, but I know that's not what I really want. I want to be unashamedly in love with you. I want to forget how I appear, and help people to see what you are. But, Father, is it all right for others to see the untidy mess that my life becomes sometimes? Do you mind that I can never satisfactorily represent you? I hope you and I will always be working on the garbage disposal, but in the meantime I'll just have to turn on the kitchen light and trust that, if I'm not ashamed of you, you won't be ashamed of me. Amen.

What is sin?

Then Jesus cried out, 'When a man believes in me, he does not believe in me only, but in the one who sent me. When he looks at me, he sees the one who sent me. I have come into the world as a light, so that no one who believes in me should stay in darkness. As for the person who hears my words but does not keep them, I do not judge him. For I did not come to judge the world, but to save it. There is a judge for the one who rejects me and does not accept my words; that very word which I spoke will condemn him at the last day. For I did not speak of my own accord, but the Father who sent me commanded me what to say and how to say it. I know that his command leads to eternal life. So whatever I say is just what the Father has told me to say.'

JOHN 12:44–50

I don't think I've ever genuinely faced the implications of what Jesus is saying here. He is stating, quite unequivocally, that when we look at him we see the one who sent him. The things that he says and the things that he does are direct acts of obedience to the Father.

If I accept that Jesus was without sin (and I do indeed accept exactly that), then I must also believe that every recorded act and word of his was right and proper in the eyes of God. This is likely to make an honest scrutiny of the Gospels extremely interesting and revealing. It is possible that, as a result, I shall be led towards a redefinition of my personal concept of sin. The idea frightens me a little, but never mind. Let's take a brief look at the 'sins' of Jesus.

First of all, there's the incident at Passover time when the twelve-year-old Jesus was taken up to Jerusalem by his parents. After the feast was over, Mary and Joseph travelled a whole day's journey towards home before discovering that their son was not with them. They assumed, as Bridget and I have assumed so many times with our own children, that Jesus was happily lumped in with cousins and friends of his own age. After all, this whole homeward procession would have been a sort of first-century, mobile Spring Harvest. The frightened parents hurried back to Jerusalem, and it was only after three days of what must have been agonizing worry that they found the boy in the temple, astonishing everyone with the maturity of his conversation. Dear Mary, worn out by four sleepless nights and a constant procession of horrible imaginings, lines up with every parent who has ever lived when she says, 'Son, why have you treated us like this?'

Nothing changes very much, does it?

I don't know about you, but I've never been very impressed by the line that Jesus came out with at this point, about how obvious it was that he should be in his Father's house, especially as—the Bible tells us—his bleary-eyed mum and dad hadn't the faintest idea what he was talking about. In some ways this encounter is fascinatingly reminiscent of modern ones—wide-eyed child amazed that foolish parent is unable to do a small thing like reading his mind, parent equally puzzled by obtuse child's failure to adopt an adult perspective. All of us parents (and children) have been there.

I do hope Jesus said *something* nice to his weary guardians. I expect he did. We know that he went back home with them, and toed the line from that point onwards. Turned out a very decent fellow, apparently.

So, does this story offer divine permission for twelve-year-olds to desert their families and spend three days doing what they feel like doing, regardless of how it will affect other people? Of course not. I don't subscribe at all to the view that Mary and Joseph brought the problem upon themselves through carelessness. The situation is just too grindingly familiar for that to be the case. Jesus caused his mother and father an enormous amount of worry and heartache when he disappeared. Was that all right, or not? Was it a sin? As I have already said, I firmly believe that Jesus was sinless, but if that act of apparent thoughtlessness and lack of concern was not a sin, what was it? That was only one of the incidents that might cause us some disquiet.

Was it a sin to kill an innocent fig tree with a curse when it didn't bear fruit, just to make a point? And what about all those pigs who were drowned because there were no other suitable receptacles for evil spirits hanging about? The Green Party would certainly have had something to say about both of those incidents, wouldn't they?

There's more.

Jesus cleared undesirables from the temple courtyard, not by loving exhortation, but by the violent application of a knotted rope to their persons; he called Peter, one of his closest followers, 'Satan' when Peter was trying to be supportive; he approved the use of valuable ointment on himself, saying that the poor were always around but he wasn't; he was extremely abusive to members of one important section of the community who disagreed with what he was doing; he made what sounds very much like a racist remark to a Greek woman who asked for help; he didn't raise a miracle-working finger to save his cousin John from imprisonment and death at the hands of Herod; and, finally, on the cross, he seemed—for a time at least—to lose his faith altogether.

I could, of course, assemble a correspondingly bizarre list of occasions when Jesus displayed compassion and forgiveness with the same kind of eccentric inappropriateness. But that only makes it more confusing—doesn't it?

Personally, I think it becomes much easier to understand, not more difficult.

As soon as we stop defining sin as a list of rules that tells us what we should and should not do, and redefine it (using Jesus' criterion) as anything that does not accurately reflect what the Father is doing or saying or commanding *in the particular situation we are in*, then the whole thing begins to look more dangerous and much more exciting.

Each church and denomination and breakaway group yearns to write a definitive rule-book. Some do it. They stagnate and die eventually, still believing that they are alive. And the Bible is not a rule-book. It is a book about the living God. In it we certainly do learn that the fundamental rules and demands of loving relationship will never be altered. Of course they won't. We know that. But equally we learn that the creative and ingenious qualities of the God who makes all things new are eternally present. He is the one who interprets to us the active language of love in this mess that the world has become. We are the ones who, if we really want to follow in the footsteps of Jesus, will simply do what we are told. Sometimes we may be very surprised at the things we are asked to do.

I would dare to suggest that Jesus' three-day absence in Jerusalem was no different, on one level, from the juvenile excesses that most of us have indulged in and suffered from. This was Jesus learning how to balance the powerful and all-absorbing attraction that his Father's business held for him (even at the age of twelve), with the needs and expectations of the people who loved him and had been given responsibility for his care and safety.

God learning how to be man—listening to God.

Jesus wasn't concerned with the admiration of men and women. He never committed a sin in his life. He just did what he saw his Father doing, and said what he heard his Father saying. In the end, it led to the cross.

Pray with me

Lord Jesus, you were very brave. You did what your Father wanted, whatever anyone else thought about it. That must have been so tough. The very people you'd come to save deserted you, ridiculed you, and finally killed you.

Look, Lord, I really want to get into this more dynamic, positive way of following, but I'm a bit nervous about where it will take me. If I do commit myself to the leading of the Holy Spirit, isn't there a chance I shall lose a few friends? You did, didn't you? Might I not end up in some strange situations? You did, didn't you? Lead me gently, Lord. Help me to listen—I want to come with you, but I am frightened. Amen.

I just can't...

Jesus knew that the Father had put all things under his power, and that he had come from God and was returning to God; so he got up from the meal, took off his outer clothing, and wrapped a towel round his waist. After that, he poured water into a basin and began to wash his disciples' feet, drying them with the towel that was wrapped round him. He came to Simon Peter, who said to him, 'Lord, are you going to wash my feet?' Jesus replied, 'You do not realize now what I am doing, but later you will understand.' 'No,' said Peter, 'you shall never wash my feet.' Jesus answered, 'Unless I wash you, you have no part with me.' 'Then, Lord,' Simon Peter replied, 'not just my feet but my hands and my head as well!' Jesus answered, 'A person who has had a bath needs only to wash his feet; his whole body is clean. And you are clean, though not every one of you.' For he knew who was going to betray him, and that was why he said not every one was clean.

JOHN 13:3–11

I never cease to be amazed by the power of inhibition. I have seen it in others and been affected by it myself. Crucial letters written but not posted, with the direst consequences. Important relationships seriously damaged by the dread of using a telephone. A season of sport lost when the fear of rejection makes it impossible to attend a first meeting. There's a lot of it about.

It's time for another piece of self-revelation. If you laugh, I shall come right out of this page and pull your nose. Here's my problem.

I hate feet.

I've always hated feet. My friend Jenny, who's a librarian, hates feet too. We sometimes sit darkly over coffee in my kitchen, sharing our mutual problem. It's good to know someone else who really understands. Jenny and I may start a Feet Haters Anonymous group if the interest is there. I stay as far away from my own feet as possible. Actually, now I think about it, I *do* like very small children's feet—little fat packets of foot. They're all right. But no others. Feet—ugh!

I remember being at a big meeting once, where Clive Calver (who should have known better, being secretary of whichever Christian Building Society it was) told the assembled masses that we were all going to wash each other's feet. I would have killed to get out of that hall. If any crinkly-eyed steward had come near me with washing equipment I would have emptied the bowl over his head, smothered him with the towel, and made a run for it. I was just lining up the large lady next to me to use as a human trampoline to get out of the row I was in, when Calver announced that he had only been joking.

Joking? About feet? That's sick. You just don't joke about feet. War, famine, plague, death—you can joke all you like about lighter subjects, but feet? Never!

I wonder if I've said enough for you to understand why this passage has never been an easy one for me. I have this awful mental picture of Jesus approaching me with his bowl of water to perform one of the greatest symbolic acts in the whole of the New Testament, and me bleating plaintively, 'Actually, I'd rather not really, if you don't mind. I've always hated feet.'

Then he would say, as he said to Peter, 'Unless I wash you, you have no part with me.'

'Even so,' I'd reply, in a strangled, panic-stricken voice, 'I'd rather not take my socks off.'

Behind all this nonsense there is a real fear in me, a small bobbing panic. Esau sold his birthright for a bowl of soup, because, at that moment, he allowed his hunger to dominate his sense. So *much* given away and lost for so very little.

My fear is that some trivial obsession or embarrassment or dread or appetite, or perhaps even a principle, will rise up at a crucial moment and choke my response to the open-hearted generosity of God. Thank goodness he's a Father and not a cold, unsympathetic judge.

Failed fathers?

It was the day of Preparation of Passover Week, about the sixth hour. 'Here is your king,' Pilate said to the Jews. But they shouted, 'Take him away! Take him away! Crucify him!' 'Shall I crucify your king?' Pilate asked. 'We have no king but Caesar,' the chief priests answered. Finally Pilate handed him over to them to be crucified. So the soldiers took charge of Jesus. Carrying his own cross, he went out to the place of the Skull (which in Aramaic is called Golgotha). Here they crucified him, and with him two others—one on each side and Jesus in the middle.

JOHN 19:14–18

Dear God,

Nothing good about Good Friday, eh?

Listen—when I was tall, skinny and eighteen, I left home in Tunbridge Wells to do an acting course at the Bristol Old Vic Theatre School. Well, you know that, of course, but if I take too much notice of your omniscience, I shall end up not telling you anything at all, and that would be a shame for both of us. I was horribly lonely, lost and disorganized during my first term, and you didn't seem to help much. Do you remember how I used to lie on the bed at my lodgings and implore you to say something, or materialize, or do anything really, just to show that you cared?

I made such a twit of myself that term, didn't I? I used to carry a big black Bible around with me like a magic talisman, and tell everyone I met that your constant presence in my life was a source of unutterable joy. Then I'd go home to that miserable little room of mine and die a thousand solitary deaths because you seemed to have stayed behind in Tunbridge Wells when I left. I found it very hard to forgive you for deserting me like that. There was I telling people about you all day— bending the truth to protect your reputation, and you were off, goodness knows where, doing something else that didn't involve me.

I cried sometimes, God. Do you hear me—I *cried*.

Anyway, I didn't mean to go on quite so much about that. What I was going to say was that while I was in Bristol I did something very difficult. I've only done a few very difficult things. The most difficult was giving up smoking when I'd reached sixty a day in 1981. But this came a pretty close second. I can hardly write about it even now.

I sat down at my small, rickety table and wrote a letter to my father (you know what a sprint through molasses that relationship was), saying all the things that I thought he would like to hear from his son—thanking him for help and guidance, that sort of stuff. I can't begin to tell you how hard it was to put those words down on paper, and I realize now why it was so very tough. It was because, by and large, what I was writing wasn't true, any more than the things I told people about my experience of you were true.

Why do I specialize in defending father-figures? I don't know. You tell me. You're the omniscient one.

Listen, I want to say something. Now that I'm still tall, but over-weight and forty-five years old, and I'm supposed to be writing about Good Friday, I want to write this letter—a more honest letter—to you, my heavenly Father, to say that I understand a little better these days. You see, I've had children of my own since then, so I know just a little of the weight of fatherhood now. I love my four kids, and I've felt such heartache when they look at me with bewilderment and reproach because I've done or allowed something unpleasant for reasons that they can't understand.

I want to be able to forgive my earthly father, and be at peace with his memory. Please allow me to forgive you for the pain of those days in Bristol. I know you won't mind, even though you didn't do anything wrong.

I only want to tell the truth now. The crowds shouted, 'CRUCIFY HIM!' and you had to let it happen.

Thank you for letting it happen.

Yours sincerely,

Adrian

Pray with me

Father,
Do I hurt you with my fear?
Do I cut you with my cries of desolation?
Do you sigh and shake your head when I cannot understand?
Do you long to make it better?
Do you seriously consider abandoning your principles?
Do you sleep?
Do you lie awake and think of me?
Does your pain roll across creation like thunder?
Is it really finished?
Daddy, won't it be good when it is? Amen.

When the morning comes

Later, Joseph of Arimathea asked Pilate for the body of Jesus. Now Joseph was a disciple of Jesus, but secretly because he feared the Jews. With Pilate's permission, he came and took the body. He was accompanied by Nicodemus, the man who earlier had visited Jesus at night. Nicodemus brought a mixture of myrrh and aloes, about seventy-five pounds. Taking Jesus' body, the two of them wrapped it, with the spices, in strips of linen. This was in accordance with Jewish burial customs. At the place where Jesus was crucified, there was a garden, and in the garden a new tomb, in which no one had ever been laid. Because it was the Jewish day of Preparation and since the tomb was near by, they laid Jesus there.

JOHN 19:38–42

Here is a scenario familiar to many of us.

You wake abruptly in the middle of the night because of a nightmare, or because of strange, unidentifiable noises from the well of darkness that is the rest of the house, and you know beyond all question that nothing short of a threat to the lives of your family could make you get out of bed to risk the perils of the unknown. Rigid with apprehension, eyes bulging and ears straining, you lie and wait for sleep to blot out fear.

In the morning, light streams through your bedroom window, warm familiar sounds of birds twittering mindlessly and dogs trying to eat postmen drift in from the outside world, and suddenly the horrors of the previous night seem absolutely ridiculous. You are certain that if the same thing ever happened again you would leap out of bed as soon as you woke, and tackle the puny unknown with defiant unconcern. How foolish you were to give in to fear so easily.

All a load of rubbish, of course, because the next time you wake in the middle of the night you feel just as frightened, and you give in just as easily. Well, I do anyway.

That's why I can identify so easily with these two chaps, Joseph and Nicodemus. They had both cowered under the sheets of public non-involvement while Jesus was alive, and now, I guess, they had just about reached the 'How foolish we were to give in to fear so easily' stage. Perhaps they were engaged in the following sort of dialogue as the burial reached its conclusion:

J: I don't know why I didn't just come right out with it while he was alive. If the whole thing started again now, which, of course, it won't *(they both shake their heads sadly)*, I'd be right there beside him. Wouldn't care who knew—wouldn't bother me at all.

N: They could flog *me* if they wanted—no problem.

J: Me too. I'd welcome it. Let 'em do their worst. 'Flog on!' That's what I'd say.

N: Kicking, beating, crucifixion even—laugh in their faces, I would. 'Ha, ha, ha!' I'd go.

J: That would upset 'em!

N: That would show 'em!
(Reflective pause)

J: I'll tell you something.

N: What?

J: You'll think I'm silly.

N: No, go on.

J: I almost wish—don't laugh—I almost wish he'd come back to life so that we could follow him to the death. All out in the open. We'd get it right next time, wouldn't we?

N: Wouldn't we just! Wouldn't we *just*! Still, there we are. Can't turn the clock back, can you?

J: Nope! Ah, well, see you Sunday?

N: Yep—see you Sunday...

I don't know how these two did cope with the reappearance of Jesus, but I do know that human beings don't change very much, and that's why the Holy Spirit needed to come. With the Spirit of God inhabiting their lives, Joseph and Nicodemus would have access to a power greater than their fears and weaknesses. It cannot be repeated too often that Jesus wanted to go so that the Spirit could come. That same Spirit is with us today, and only his intervention in our lives will enable us to rise above habits of fear and failure. It will never be easy, but it will be *possible*, and that, I can assure you, is a miracle.

Pray with me

Father, the longer I live, the more I understand that no earthly optimism or effort can even begin to take the place of the power that the Holy Spirit brings into our lives. Fill us with the supernatural grace that changed Peter from a man who said and did the wrong things, into a bold and effective spokesman for God at Pentecost. When the Spirit comes, weak people find amazing strength; mouthy people quieten down; timid people become bold; uncertain people are sure, and frightened people do brave things, even when it's dark.

We need you, Holy Spirit. We cry out for you to come. Come and fill us now as we call on you. Amen.

All in order

Early on the first day of the week, while it was still dark, Mary Magdalene went to the tomb and saw that the stone had been removed from the entrance... On the evening of that first day of the week, when the disciples were together, with the doors locked for fear of the Jews, Jesus came and stood among them and said, 'Peace be with you!'

JOHN 20:1, 19

English was my best subject at school, and mathematics was my worst. Like Linus, I'm unable to tell people I can stand on my own two feet until I've counted them, just to make sure. That may be something of an exaggeration, but it is true that my brain seized up when problems involving quadratic equations were fed into it, and I was never able to get any further.

Recently, though, I've been reading about something called 'chaos theory', and, because it was woven into the fabric of a popular paperback, I managed to understand as much as a tenth of what I read. Mathematicians who work in this field claim a greater concern than is traditional with describing things that exist in the real world (unlike a number of theologians).

Chaos theory says, among other things, that simple systems can produce complex behaviour. It might appear possible, for instance, to predict the exact destination of a snooker ball after it had cannoned around a table for an hour or so (if that could be made to happen), simply by calculating angles and distances. Theoretically it is possible, but in fact it won't be long before tiny imperfections in the ball and indentations in the surface of the table overpower those careful calculations. The (apparently) simple system of a snooker ball on a table has unpredictable behaviour.

Perhaps humanity has always sensed and dreaded this inherent unpredictability of life. Social systems might appear simple, but they never are. Nothing is. The wild randomness of existence on this planet is one of the deepest fears of Humankind Without God. Rituals, novels, drama, philosophies, laws, religion and fairy tales that end happily ever after are all strategies we have devised to convince ourselves that simple, predictable patterns of living are possible. Two major wars in the 20th century should persuade us that we are kidding ourselves. We know we are adrift.

But these strivings towards meaning are also, I believe, instinctive responses from a race that was originally made in the image of God. We have known in our hearts that it shouldn't be random—that the world was always supposed to make sense, and that something has gone very wrong.

I used to feel slightly annoyed by the way in which Jesus seemed to slavishly perform acts or say things so that prophecies could be seen to be fulfilled, but I can see now the need for the logic or pattern of the life of God to be visible in history, encouraging men and women to believe that destiny can be controlled.

On that dark Sunday morning, Mary could never have guessed the cosmic significance of the empty tomb. When Jesus rose from the dead the ancient engines of order were fired once more and, in his body on earth, chaos was defeated.

And what a wonderful moment for Jesus and his disciples. Neither locks nor fears could withstand the peace and security that the risen Saviour brought, and still brings, to his people. It is the peace of knowing that, however rough the road may need to be (and it often is), we shall indeed, in the most real sense, live happily ever after.

Say a final prayer with me

There are times, Father, when the apparent lack of order in this world causes us to panic. We feel like survivors of some great Titanic-like disaster, floating around on little rafts on our own, or with a few other bewildered ex-passengers. Now we want to celebrate the fact that you have a strong grip on creation and on us. We praise you for the gift of Jesus, who restored the rule of love to this wrecked world, and assured us that he would be with us always. We lift our troubled eyes to you, Father, and smile as we express our gratitude to you for being in charge. We offer our fears to you and trust you with them. Thank you for organizing a future that makes sense. Amen.

You may be interested to know that Adrian Plass is a regular contributor to *New Daylight*, BRF's popular series of Bible reading notes. *New Daylight* is ideal for those looking for a fresh, devotional approach to reading and understanding the Bible. Each issue covers four months of daily Bible reading and reflection with each day offering a Bible passage (text included), helpful comment and a prayer or thought for the day ahead.

New Daylight is written by a gifted team of contributors including Adrian Plass, Margaret Cundiff, David Winter, Rob Gillion, Rachel Boulding, Peter Graves, Helen Julian CSF, David Spriggs, Jenny Robertson and Veronica Zundel.

New Daylight is also available in large print and on cassette for the visually impaired.

NEW DAYLIGHT SUBSCRIPTIONS

❏ I would like to give a gift subscription
(please complete both name and address sections below)
❏ I would like to take out a subscription myself
(complete name and address details only once)

This completed coupon should be sent with appropriate payment to BRF. Alternatively, please write to us quoting your name, address, the subscription you would like for either yourself or a friend (with their name and address), the start date and credit card number, expiry date and signature if paying by credit card.

Gift subscription name _____

Gift subscription address _____

_____ Postcode _____

Please send to the above, beginning with the May/September 2002/January 2003 issue:

(please tick box)	UK	SURFACE	AIR MAIL
NEW DAYLIGHT	❏ £10.50	❏ £11.85	❏ £14.10
NEW DAYLIGHT 3-year sub	❏ £26.50		

Please complete the payment details below and send your coupon, with appropriate payment to: **BRF, First Floor, Elsfield Hall, 15–17 Elsfield Way, Oxford OX2 8FG**

Your name _____

Your address _____

_____ Postcode _____

Total enclosed £ _____ (cheques should be made payable to 'BRF')

Payment by cheque ❏ postal order ❏ Visa ❏ Mastercard ❏ Switch ❏

Card number: ☐☐☐☐☐☐☐☐☐☐☐☐☐☐☐☐

Expiry date of card: ☐☐☐☐ Issue number (Switch): ☐☐☐☐

Signature (essential if paying by credit/Switch card) _____

NB: BRF notes are also available from your local Christian bookshop. **BRF is a Registered Charity**